How to
Value & Sell
your Business

For my three girls: Tracey, Holly and Lucy.
With love.

How to
Value & Sell
your Business

The essential guide to preparing,
valuing and selling a
company for maximum profit

Andrew Heslop

RECOMMENDED BY
INSTITUTE OF DIRECTORS

KOGAN
PAGE

London and Philadelphia

This book has been endorsed by the Institute of Directors.

The endorsement is given to selected Kogan Page books which the IoD recognizes as being of specific interest to its members and providing them with up-to-date, informative and practical resources for creating business success. Kogan Page books endorsed by the IoD represent the most authoritative guidance available on a wide range of subjects including management, finance, marketing, training and HR.

The views expressed in this book are those of the author and are not necessarily the same as those of the Institute of Directors.

Publisher's note

Every possible effort has been made to ensure that the information contained in this book is accurate at the time of going to press, and the publishers and author cannot accept responsibility for any errors or omissions, however caused. No responsibility for loss or damage occasioned to any person acting, or refraining from action, as a result of the material in this publication can be accepted by the editor, the publisher or any of the authors.

First published in Great Britain and the United States in 2008 by Kogan Page Limited

120 Pentonville Road
London N1 9JN
United Kingdom
www.kogan-page.co.uk

525 South 4th Street, #241
Philadelphia PA 19147
USA

© Andrew Heslop, 2008

The right of Andrew Heslop to be identified as the author of this work has been asserted by him in accordance with the Copyright, Designs and Patents Act 1988.

ISBN 978 0 7494 5117 2

British Library Cataloguing-in-Publication Data

A CIP record for this book is available from the British Library.

Library of Congress Cataloging-in-Publication Data
Heslop, Andrew.
    How to value and sell your business : the essential guide to preparing, valuing and selling a company for maximum profit / Andrew Heslop.
        p. cm.
    Includes index.
    ISBN 978-0-7494-5117-2
    1. Sale of business enterprises. 2. Business enterprises--Valuation. I. Title.
    HD1393.25.H45 2007
    658.1'64--dc22
                                                            2007041519

Typeset by JS Typesetting Ltd, Porthcawl, Mid Glamorgan
Printed and bound in Great Britain by Bell & Bain Ltd, Glasgow

CHESHAM

BECAUSE YOU ONLY SELL
YOUR BUSINESS ONCE

And you know that it's a scarce resource.

Why pay someone to produce the buyers?
Perhaps you should talk to Chesham.

With a wide range of confidential briefs from
PLC's, foreign multinational and private equity
houses as well as MBI teams, all of whom are
looking to buy successful, private companies for
between £1 million and £50 million, we ought
to be able to help.

So, if you're thinking of selling your business and
would like a service which enhances the price and
minimises the cost to you, contact us for a
confidential discussion.

CHESHAM
AMALGAMATIONS
The first name in merger broking

Telephone: 020 7060 0363
www.CheshamAmalgamations.com

Chesham's merger-making builds on its history
By Tom Leeds

Goodwill is always difficult to value, and is often one of the more contentious issues when companies are sold. When Philip Craig and Jonathan Reddaway bought control of Chesham Amalgamations and Investments, one of the oldest and best respected names in merger broking in the UK, they were faced with just this problem. Merger broking, the art of bringing a willing vendor and buyer together under the best circumstances, has many intangibles. But financially, it could be argued, the business is only as good as the next deal. How much should one pay for history?

Chesham has an extraordinary genesis. It was founded in 1962 by management consultant Francis Singer, in partnership with Nicholas Stacey, a fellow Austro-Hungarian who was then Director of the Chartered Institute of Secretaries, naming the company after their address at 36 Chesham Place, W1.
Stacey introduced Sir Miles Thomas, later Lord Thomas of Remenham, who had been chairman of BOAC (now British Airways) and the National Savings Board.

Two years later, in 1964, a new Labour government recognized the need to revitalize Britain's flagging industrial base. The Industrial Reorganisation Corporation, whose brief was to promote mergers in industries ranging from pumps to textiles, found Chesham's knowledge of these sectors useful, resulting in significant business for the broker.

By 1969, with the arrival of Sir Neil Shields as a third executive director, Chesham's revenues were strong enough to enable it to make its own bid for Central and Sherwood Trust, a listed company involved in print and publishing. The merger of CST and Chesham however created conflicts of interest, with clients fearing that CST would keep the best pickings, and Chesham's brokers becoming exasperated by having to navigate between these conflicts.

Singer, Stacey and Sir Neil eventually retired in 1983, Lord Thomas having died a few years previously. John (later Lord) Eden, a nephew of the prime minister, became chairman, and decided to sell Chesham, which didn't fit with CST's expanding engineering activities. It was bought by Grovewood Securities, a subsidiary of Eagle Star, and one of Chesham's more successful clients. When Eagle Star in turn was acquired by British American Tobacco, Chesham had become an almost invisible entity in BAT's massive operations.

In 1985, John Fleming, who had built a successful career in South Africa based on the PE Consulting Group franchise, decided to move to England, and in partnership with Jim Paton, who had been involved in acquisitions at Grovewood Securities, organised the purchase of Chesham from BAT. Paton died in the mid 1990s, and Fleming retired in 2004, when the business was sold to Jonathan Reddaway and Philip Craig.

Reddaway and Craig are an interesting contrast to the establishment directors of Chesham's past. Reddaway is a civil engineer who has worked in Africa and the Middle East. Craig is a graduate of the London Business School with a background in corporate finance. Both worked with Chesham for nearly ten years before acquiring it, so they are imbued with the firm's ethic of total integrity, with strict rules on client interests, fees and confidentiality. "Our clients typically have sales of between £10m and £50m," says Reddaway, "though we have handled both larger and smaller deals. We find that the major City institutions do an excellent job for their large clients, but the smaller ones tend to get fairly short shrift. We can give these clients very close attention, and they often end up as friends. The problems of selling smaller companies are every bit as complex as selling large ones, and they need the attention which firms like ours can provide."

The Chesham team now consists of eleven brokers and consultants, with high level experience of working in, or running, businesses in investment banking, the hitech sector, defence, oil, energy, engineering, banking, media, and financial services. A former client also provides advice and support in legal and financial matters as well as in the post-deal phase, when press or media concerns are important. Reddaway explains that although this team experience is important, Chesham can only function efficiently if its research and control systems generate a corporate memory which all its brokers can access.

"We realize that information is the key to our business, and we have a quite sophisticated computer set-up, both to provide data and also to collect information about deals and our own activities. This enables us to function as a virtual office, with information flowing to and from a number of different sites."

Two recent deals, the media merger of Ideas Eurobrand and Cascaid Group, and the private equity buy-in at engineers Fin Machine Company, have strengthened the belief of Chesham's new owners that the systems approach of the 21st century can add to the historical approach of contacts and experience. So what was Chesham's goodwill worth when they bought the business? Craig smiles and says simply, "A good deal. And you can read that in any way you like."

For more information on Chesham see its website at
www.CheshamAmalgamations.com

Contents

Realising the value of manufacturing companies in the UK

There is a widespread misconception that the perceived decline of British manufacturing industry negatively affects the attractiveness, and therefore sale value, of owner-manager UK based businesses. Our experience is that reality and perception are poles apart. Whilst long term decline may be the unfortunate trend for large mass-production companies (typically in the automotive sector), it is certainly not the case for niche manufacturers: we can confirm there is a healthy demand for small- and medium-sized businesses throughout many parts of the manufacturing sector. The misconception must be overcome so as to achieve the best value for the departing owner.

At Hornblower we invest time to understand your business – assessing its performance and prospects. As sector-specialists, we help present your business in the strongest possible light to a targeted range of potential investors.

Most people only sell one business in a lifetime, and it is crucial to maximize the results. Hornblower helps sellers achieve best value through careful construction of the sales prospectus, accurate valuation of the business's tangible and intangible assets, and careful targeting of prospective purchasers. Such an approach requires an objectivity and time investment that an existing owner, immersed in the day-to-day running of the company, may not have. Preparing a business for sale and handling the complexities of the disposal process requires both experience and significant resources – at a time when the owner manager can least afford to restrict their involvement in managing their business. Hornblower's extensive experience in market research, identifying competitors, evaluating existing market penetration and realistic projected growth, and identifying prospective buyers means that it is well placed to help private companies achieve maximum sale value – whilst providing support to overstretched owner managers.

Hornblower specialises in the industrial sector, and has much experience in supporting small- and medium-sized enterprises. Our expanding client base includes both UK based businesses eager to expand through local acquisition as well as an international network of parties interested in British investment opportunities, from the EU to Australia and South Africa. As our management team has extensive international experience, we are well placed to help private companies exploit sale opportunities with parties based in the UK and abroad.

Despite press reports of increasingly gloomy economic indicators, manufacturing in the UK represents a sound investment for buyers, and a profitable exit opportunity for sellers. At Hornblower, our core competence lies in bringing the two parts together into a successful and attractive deal.

For further information, please contact Hornblower Business Brokers on **+44 (0) 20 8090 9380** or email **ask@hornblower-businesses.co.uk** Website: **www.hornblower-businesses.co.uk**

LAWRENCE & CO

BUSINESS TRANSFER AGENTS

Established 1994

Owners wishing to sell contact
Mark Walton MBA DipFS FCIB MNAEA MICBA
In strict confidence

Telephone: (0870) 6092170   Fax: (01444 440357)
www.lawrenceco.net

Successfully Selling Businesses since 1994

We are experts in obtaining the best possible deal and once the deal is agreed we guide you on a path that avoids pitfalls and potential problems. Working closely with all the parties and solicitors in the transaction we proactively guide the process to ensure the sale completes as quickly as possible.

There are many issues to consider when selling or buying a business and to guide all our clients we have produced a Step by Step Guide to Selling and Buying a Business which can be obtained free of charge on request.

If you are considering a sale of your business and would like a no obligation valuation of your business, please phone us on 0870 6092170.

Lawrence & Co. is the Premier Independent **Business Transfer** Agency specialising in the Sale of **Dry Cleaning, Launderette and Laundry Businesses** and business property sales across the UK.

Established in 1994 we have built up an excellent reputation for professionalism and integrity with both **sellers and buyers** of dry cleaners businesses, laundries and launderettes. Our expertise within the dry cleaning and laundry industry means that we are well known and the first point of contact for buyers seeking businesses for sale.

Selling your business is one of the most important decisions you'll ever make. Buying or selling a business is likely to be something you do only once during your lives. We are able to call on a wealth of expertise and experience in all manner of business sales, while recognising the need to provide a highly personalized and individual approach. We offer advice & assistance to secure the best possible outcome for you.

We always aim to provide an unrivalled service of quality and value, and wherever possible, exceed the expectations of our clients. We are constantly seeking new ways to add value and speed up the sale process for all our clients. We have managed the successful sale of numerous businesses; and are dedicated to helping our clients maximise the price achieved for their business with the added reassurance of our 'no sale – no fee' guarantee.

We can market your business without your employees, customers or competitors knowing that the business is for sale. We can discuss the fundamentals of your business and of the proposed sale without releasing your business name until you the seller are happy to do so.

Grown it? Sell it?

Growing a company, although rewarding, can be a long, arduous and time consuming task. Is now the time to consider passing the workload on and enjoying the fruits of your labour?

If it could be, why not talk to us to find out more about how we can help your business sell and achieve a maximised sale price? We help more privately owned businesses sell than anyone else, achieving average sale prices for our clients' businesses which are 2.5 times more than the lowest offer received.

Last year over 2,500 business owners attended our seminars and over 1000 spoke to us personally about maximising the sale price of their business. To meet and talk to one of our Business Managers confidentially simply call **01635 299616** or visit **www.bcmscorporate.com** for more information and to book into a seminar.

BCMS Corporate Ltd, Plantagenet House, Kingsclere, Newbury, Berkshire RG20 4SW

Selling your business for its maximum value

There is an approach to valuing private companies that is consistently applied but is fundamentally flawed. This approach involves assessing a company's average underlying operating profit and applying a multiple to achieve a value.

If a company has an average operating profit (after adjustments and tax) of, for example, £500,000 and a multiple of seven is applied then the value for the 'going concern' is assumed to be £3.5 million. This value will ensure a return on investment in seven years. At BCMS Corporate we strongly contend with this mindset because we can prove that the value of a business is rooted in the motives of the acquirer and not in simple multiples of (historic) profit.

At BCMS Corporate we hold negotiative dialogue with 230 (av.) potential acquirers for every one of our clients and a rigorous qualification process reduces this to 6 (av.) companies that are serious enough for us to invite to make competitive offers. On average the highest offer we receive will be 2.5 times the lowest. If the value of a business was all about multiples of historic profit then offers would be very similar but we find this rarely occurs.

So, why is one company prepared to pay 2.5 times more than another? Simply because they are buying for different motives. Motives of acquirers ultimately determine value, which in turn means that it is almost impossible to value a business before taking it to market. A business owner may be able to determine a 'walk-away' price or even an aspirational price, but never a sale price. A company is always worth what someone is prepared to pay for it.

Examples of reasons for making an acquisition include: A complementary product/service supplier which will benefit from being able to cross sell to both sets of clients, an overseas company looking to gain access to a new market and a competitor seeking to make savings in production and eliminate a competitor thus releasing downward pressure on product price.

Risk also plays a part in influencing offers. A company that generates cash or enjoys guaranteed income streams may be seen as an acquisition with lower risk.

So how is it possible to ensure an acquirer bids according to motives rather than multiples? The answer to this lies in selling future potential and generating a competitive bidding environment.

Selling future potential and establishing choice

At BCMS Corporate we produce, a 'Step change' business plan for our clients. This plan considers how the business will be performing in three years under each potential acquirer's ownership. How will the business have grown when the new owner has applied their resources to the business? The results of this plan exert a significant influence over the sale price making this the most important document produced for our clients.

One important message that our Negotiation Director regularly reminds us of is that we should negotiate from what at first glance appears to be an unreasonable position. As we have already said, selling a company on the basis of future growth rather than past performance seems unreasonable. A potential acquirer might well argue 'Why should we pay a premium price when it is our actions that generate this future growth?' Our only defense is to have a choice of acquirers. Having a choice of acquirers is the single most influential issue that affects the sale price of a company.

If the acquirer is not prepared to see value in future growth then somebody else probably will. As neither party alone brings the all the elements necessary for this future growth; both contribute and therefore both buyer and seller should benefit. Future potential is one of the most common motives for buying a company.

At BCMS we take five distinct steps to ensure that a company sells for its maximum value.

For further details visit **www.bcmscorporate.com**

How do you select a broker to manage the sale of your business?

A good broker should provide an honest valuation, a high probability of achieving that value through a comprehensive and proactive marketing campaign and above all represent an organisation that instils trust and confidence that the sale will be achieved.

Every business owner wants to maximise the amount they sell their business for and can therefore be attracted to brokers who provide high valuations. Unfortunately valuing and selling are two different things and it is a little known fact that, where businesses are advertised with an asking price, the average realisation is around 40% of that price.

Churchfield recognises that it is a major life changing decision to sell a business and that decision will be based in part on the valuation received prior to marketing. Our approach is to provide an honest valuation based on the information obtained from the vendor and not based on winning the business at all costs. We invest considerable time and care in gathering information before arriving at valuations and have an excellent record in achieving or exceeding valuations provided.

The valuation remains confidential between us and the vendor and we don't rely on advertising to sell a business. Instead we market businesses extensively to: trade buyers, using exhaustive research to determine the best possible matches; acquisitive buyers known to us or who have registered on our site; other buyers via specialist web sites, our web site and specialist publications. We produce comprehensive and detailed sales documents and manage the process to generate offers through a competitive bidding process. This approach identifies the largest number of potential buyers providing the best opportunity of selling at the highest possible price.

Trust is absolutely critical and that is why every sale is handled by one of our directors who will personally manage the process and provide guidance and support every step of the way. Although we can't take on every business that comes our way we can assure all our clients that they will get a highly professional service and can feel totally confident that the sale of their business is in safe hands.

sold

Talk to most business brokers, advisers or accountants and you will notice a lot of mysticism, confusion and jargon surrounding the selling of a business. Take away the smoke and mirrors and you will find that with thoughtful preparation, a bit of common sense and the guiding hand of an experienced broker, the process can be very rewarding and quite straight forward.

We provide unbiased, knowledgeable, common sense and specialist advice to clients large and small and have a combined business sales experience spanning thirty-two years. Having sold millions of pounds worth of businesses and worked all over the UK in nearly all sectors of industry and commerce, we have the experience you need. Visit our testimonial page on our website, www.lucasweston.com, to view examples of our many success stories.

Is our experience solely academic? Most definitely not. We have started, built, run, managed, bought and sold several of our own businesses. We are in the unique positions of knowing exactly what issues and concerns you might have because we have had to confront them too.

For more information, help and advice, you can contact us confidentially with an e-mail or a telephone call. We will do all we can to help you. No smoke. No mirrors.

▦ LUCAS & WESTON

BUSINESS SALES   MERGERS   ACQUISITIONS   ADVICE

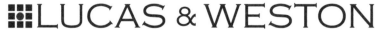

www.lucasweston.com   ask@lucasweston.com   0845 644 0266

How My Mistake Will Help You Save a Fortune
By Howard Weston

I started my first business in 1995 when commercial diving services were in great demand. From day one, we won large contracts. We were good, we grew quickly and had a fresh approach to client problems. We were also very profitable and becoming a major thorn in our competitors sides.

How much?!

Out of the blue I received a call from a rival MD with an invitation. Intrigued, I accepted. Over that lavish lunch I received an offer that would change my life. Would someone really want to buy a business only a year old? As much as I was flattered, I was also very naive. Their offer was accepted very quickly as I thought it too good to be true. I didn't question the buyer's motives or even think that others might be interested. My main focus was this lucrative offer served up on a plate.

Pulling teeth

I had a deal and felt like Richard Branson. I was out of my depth although I didn't know it. I needed help. Where do you get independent advice? How do you find an experienced guiding hand? How do you know what advice you need? I just picked a lawyer from Yellow Pages and began the process. For the next five months I learnt a new language: due-diligence, CGT, EBITDA, preference shares, earn outs, performance payments, loan notes, non-compete clauses, warranties and guarantees became my new vocabulary. Was it really this complicated to sell a business? The deal nearly collapsed on several occasions as the buyer's patience wore thin while I struggled to keep things together as well as running the business. Eventually the sale completed.

Wonderful thing, hindsight

Six months after completion I heard that the buyer had sold my business. When I learned what they received I felt sick to my stomach. How could I have not seen it? They'd identified the gem I hadn't and they knew its value along with how to capitalise on it. I'd undersold the crown jewels – significantly.

The foundations of a new career

I subsequently started and sold two further businesses. This time, having learnt the lessons from the past, I sought good advice on both occasions. I became more and more interested in the process of selling businesses. It became an obsession. I routed out information and advice from anywhere I could get it, including three years working as a broker with a national Mergers and Acquisition firm.

Lucas & Weston

Remembering the difficulty I had trying to find the right advice or just basic information, coupled with my frustration at how traditional business sales worked, I eventually quit my job and started Lucas & Weston Ltd. My vision was, and still is, to sell businesses. By applying the latest technology, cutting edge marketing and good old fashioned values such as attention to detail, hard work, integrity and professionalism we have grown steadily ever since.

Learn from my mistake

For the past twelve years I have been successfully selling businesses, representing PLC's, Limited Companies, Partnerships and Sole Traders on deals worth millions of pounds. It is easy to look back with hindsight and see the mistakes I made and how easily they could, and should, have been avoided.

If you're seriously considering the sale of your business, I'd like to share the hard won benefit of my experiences with you and help you achieve your goal. Move on to the next stage of your life – be it leisurely retirement, continued involvement or new opportunities.

To find out more please visit our website **www.lucasweston.com** where you can read testimonials and see examples of our proven track record. Alternatively, I'd be delighted to hear from you.

Howard Weston
Managing Director
Lucas & Weston Ltd
Tel: 0845 644 0266

SUCCESS

Thinking of Selling your Business?

As business transfer specialists, Stirling help business owners achieve maximum return on their investment when it is time to sell. We work on the business owner's behalf developing exit strategies, marketing the business and negotiating with prospective buyers. Whether it's a share or asset sale, you will benefit from our extensive experience and support. Your business will be marketed professionally and discretely by experts, with a high level of personal service which will not cost the earth.

- Independent valuations
- Exit strategies
- Grooming for sale
- Independent legal, pension and tax advice
- Professional Sale Memorandum, national advertising and internet promotion
- Discretion and confidentiality at all times
- Meetings and negotiations

Stirling Business Solutions Ltd   Lasyard House   Underhill Street Bridgnorth Shropshire WV16 4BB
Tel: 01746 769301   Fax: 01746 769302   Email: info@stirling-uk.com   www.stirling-uk.com

Using a Business Transfer Specialist

Most business owners will only sell a business once in a lifetime. Without previous experience, it can be a difficult, complicated and stressful process. Selling a business is a major financial decision and can be a costly one, unless opportunities for reduced taxation, pensions and other areas of financial planning are considered. Sufficient reason then for using a Business Transfer Specialist to manage the sale and maximise the financial return for the business owner.

The process of selling a business requires careful planning with special attention to marketing and presenting the company correctly, to ensure that the message reaches as many potential buyers as possible. The price and terms for the business sale need to be skilfully negotiated, keeping all options open with potential buyers, to secure the best sale for the business owner.

By appointing a Business Transfer Specialist or Broker, you stand a much greater chance of securing a higher sale price and thereby will be able to cover the sale fee several times over. Most brokers will have a database of potential investors looking for businesses for sale and they should know where to advertise a business to generate good enquiries. This is important as the value of the business is often described as being "worth as much as someone is prepared to pay for it" (despite at least 5 different valuation methods). It therefore makes sense for the broker to aim for a short list of potential buyers which will usually bring in a range of offers, some of which may be double that of others.

An important part of the sales process is the provision of useful information to the prospective buyer. The seller will need to ensure that essential information such as the Statutory Accounts, Management Accounts, Staff Records, Contracts of Employment etc are all up to date as part of their exit strategy, whilst the Business Transfer Specialist will prepare a Sale Memorandum document for the prospective buyer, once a Confidentiality Agreement has been secured.

The Sale Memorandum needs to be professionally written and presented, as this will provide a first impression to the prospective buyer. The potential buyer needs to understand exactly "what is being sold", to decide whether or not to acquire the business. No one likes time wasters, so far better to gain feedback at an early stage.

The Business Transfer Specialist should be able to provide good information to the prospective purchaser (provided by the seller) and keep a database of all potential prospects. Dealing with enquiries, Confidentiality Agreements and supplying timely information will enable the business owner to carry on running the business whilst a buyer is found.

Before appointing a Business Transfer Specialist, it is worthwhile meeting at least three brokers to compare terms of business, fee structures and to clearly understand exactly what services will be to be provided, especially when it comes to marketing. It is also worth clarifying exactly 'who' the business owner will be dealing with. Read the 'small print' on the terms of business, such as exclusivity clauses and cancellation terms. Finally, check the standard to which the Sale Memorandum document will be prepared. The business owner may have spent years developing a brand and corporate identity, presenting the business in a professional manner, so the same should be done when the time comes to sell the business.

By taking time to understand your future plans, the Broker will be able to develop an agreed exit strategy and business transfer plan to achieve a successful sale. However, the sooner you start planning for the sale the better, as the process can take up to six months to find a buyer and a further six months to complete the sale. A good Business Transfer Specialist will not charge the earth and will have a realistic view on valuation, exit options and taxation. You may only sell a business once, so it is worth getting the best advice and help available to realise your future plans.

Roger Stirling Smith FIOD - Stirling, Business Transfer Specialists

Acknowledgements

Writing a book is quite a solitary activity. However, the contents of this book could not have been written without a number of people sharing their valuable time, experience and insights. I am especially indebted to the following professionals who gave their time generously and freely: Susie Cawood of York and North Yorkshire Chamber of Commerce, Tony Tarpey of Garbutt and Elliot Accountants, Andrew Lindsay of Denison Till Solicitors, James Towler of Langleys Solicitors, Nick Darby of Denton Wilde Sapte Solicitors and David Dinsdale of Business Link.

Tony Gill openly shared details of his hugely successful business career, the detail of which would justify a book of its own. Other people who were generous with time and information include Michael Clark of EllisClark Associates, Paul Brown of the British Retail Consortium and Kit Bird, a member of the Yorkshire Association of Business Angels. I also thank Mike Buchanan, a fellow writer who sent a stream of funny e-mails to keep me amused through the process of crunching thousands of words over many weeks.

Finally, many thanks are due to my ex-business partner Ray Schofield. Without him I would have never begun the strange series of adventures that culminated in the publication of this book. Ray is perhaps the only person in the history of the world to sell a print business through a physiotherapist.

DISCLAIMER

The primary purpose of this book is to help you consider how to exit your business, and it describes the processes that might be involved. Its aim is to be helpful and to offer practical insights. All information within the book is conveyed in good faith, but for obvious reasons cannot be guaranteed to be appropriate when applied to your specific circumstances.

In many respects this is not a 'do it yourself' book. Some of the legal issues involved in planning and conducting a business sale are complex and variable. You will be advised many times during the book that you should refer to an experienced lawyer or accountant. This advice is repeated here.

Selling your business is our business.

When it comes to selling your business, you need to talk to people you can rely on to get it right. Cavendish is the UK's leading independent advisor to business vendors because that's all we do. We've found the right buyers and maximised value for some 400 businesses over the past 20 years – and we can do the same for you.

Corporate Finance Boutique of the Year 2007
– BVCA/Real Deals Private Equity Awards
– Private Equity News Awards for Excellence in Advisory Services

Cavendish Corporate Finance Limited
40 Portland Place, London W1B 1NB
Tel: +44 (0)20 7908 6000
www.cavendish.com

Unrivalled expertise in selling businesses

Authorised and regulated by the Financial Services Authority.

Cavendish

Selling Your Business Is Our Business

Cavendish Corporate Finance – the UK's leading specialist adviser to business vendors

When you are selling a business, you want the best possible deal, structured in the best possible way.

Cavendish Corporate Finance is the UK's leading independent specialist adviser to vendors of businesses.

As we act only for vendors of businesses, we avoid the conflicts of interest between purchasers and vendors experience by most other advisers, who act on both sides of deals. This allows us to focus on what really matters – managing the sale process to ensure that the best price is achieved for the vendor.

In addition to advising owners of private companies, Cavendish frequently advises major public companies and leading financial institutions. Cavendish has worked with nearly all of the major private equity houses in the UK.

Why our expertise is second to none

Fundamental to the success of a company sale is achieving effective access to a wide range of prospective purchasers. This maximises the likelihood of creating a competitive environment within the sale process and achieving a premium price.

As a leading adviser in the arena of UK company sales, Cavendish continually receives approaches from prospective purchasers. Recognising that we do not charge fees to purchasers, acquisitive companies and financial institutions are always keen to talk to Cavendish about their requirements. This has enabled us to build a unique database of potential purchasers for mid-market UK companies.

Cavendish has a strong record of identifying purchasers from outside a client's immediate market. Such purchasers are often prepared to pay a premium price to enter a new market. In such circumstances, this may avoid unnecessary contact with competitors.

Preparing your business for sale

Cavendish has built its reputation on finding the right buyer, deal and terms for its clients no matter the timescale. However, it maybe that you know you wish to sell your business at some point in the near future but do not yet have a firm exit plan.

To assist those shareholders who have the time to plan a future exit strategy, Cavendish has developed its unique Exit Review Process. This is strategically aimed at enhancing value and positioning businesses for sale during the 6-18 months prior to commencing a sale exercise.

Part of the world's leading international M&A alliance
Cavendish is a member of M&A International Inc., the world's leading international alliance of specialist mergers and acquisitions advisers.

M&A International offers the unparalleled resources of some 42 independently owned mergers and acquisitions specialists and investment banking firms in some 38 countries – covering key business centres in Europe, the Americas, Africa, Asia and the Pacific Rim.

M&A International is currently completing around 300 transactions annually, with an approximate aggregate value of US$8 billion. On average, a transaction has been closed every working day for the last 3 years.

Membership of M&A International provides Cavendish with invaluable access to overseas purchasers, which has led to a number of successful cross-border transactions.

In summary, why sell your business with Cavendish?
- We are the UK's leading specialist adviser to vendors of businesses.
- We were named Corporate Finance Boutique of the Year 2007 at both the BVCA/Real Deals Private Equity Awards and the Private Equity News Awards for Excellence in Advisory Services.
- We provide access to an extensive database of acquirers.
- We have global coverage through membership of M&A International, Inc. giving us access to a worldwide team of 400 professional advisers and sector specialists.
- We are independent and owned by our directors.
- We have a long track record, having successfully advised on some 400 company sales with an aggregate balance of £3 billion.

For more information call **+44 (0)207 908 6000** or email **info@cavendish.com**

Cavendish Corporate Finance Limited
40 Portland Place, London W1B 1NB
www.cavendish.com

Foreword

GETTING YOUR JUST REWARDS

Recent years have seen a strong market for buying and selling private companies. With both inflation and interest rates at historically low levels, and steady economic growth, there has generally been confidence in stock market flotations and ready interest from trade buyers. In short, there has been a benign environment for deals. With the recent 'credit crunch' and stock market volatility, this won't necessarily be the case going forward. As we are often reminded by financial advisers, past performance is no guarantee of future success.

But regardless of the state of the economy and the financial markets, companies are bought and sold constantly – and for a variety of reasons. Typically acquisitions are made to gain market share, achieve economies of scale or product synergy, diversify risk or ensure supplies or outlets. Sales may stem from the retirement of the owner and the realisation of investors' capital to, in some unfortunate cases, the so-called 'fire-sale' of a struggling enterprise.

Whatever their reasons for selling, *How to Value and Sell Your Business* will provide business owners with a practical, readable insight into how to maximise the valuation of their enterprise and derive the best possible return from its sale. Clear strategy, careful planning and expert advice are all needed.

Many owners of private companies only have the opportunity to sell once in a business career and it is something they cannot afford to get wrong. This book will also help them to avoid some of the stresses and strains that such a major transaction can so easily induce.

The book distils the accumulated knowledge of professional experts and the practical experience of company directors who have been through the process – and have witnessed both triumph and trauma at first hand. Their insights into the process are too valuable to be ignored.

Miles Templeman, Director General,
Institute of Directors

Introduction

VALUING AND SELLING YOUR BUSINESS

How much is your business worth? If you are able to answer this question with a sensible and tangible figure you are already well ahead of most business owners. How much your business is worth is inextricably linked to the question 'Who will buy your business?' Straightforward questions often lead to complicated answers but this book aims to demystify the process of valuing and selling a business. The ideas presented will be useful and direct, and based on real-life experiences of myself and many other people.

The book has four high-level objectives:

1. To help you assess how much your business is worth (or may be worth in future).
2. To provide ideas and enthusiasm for the process of identifying who will buy your business.
3. To provide ideas for maximizing the sale price achieved.
4. To help you plan and manage all aspects of the sale process.

Achieving an accurate assessment of the value of your business is not just important when the time comes to sell. If you are raising capital (borrowing money) through a bank or other investment company, it will probably want to assess the value of your business as it stands. This figure represents a tangible asset that can be used as security in the event that things do not go according to plan. Understanding the value of your business is important whether or not you have firm plans to sell in the near future.

So how much is your business worth? Well, businesses, like cars, holidays, houses, horses and anything else you care to mention are worth what someone is prepared to pay. Although this answer is entirely accurate it does not have the advantage of being remotely useful. It's like when an economist draws a multi-coloured supply and demand graph but we still don't know the price of petrol next April. A more sensible answer to the question would be 'It depends.' It depends on the model or approach you take in valuing your business. It also depends on who you ask. And when you ask them.

For example, your accountant might say something along the lines of 'Your business is worth its net present value (as determined by the balance sheet) plus the net present value of all future known revenues.' Two things to note here. First, he or she is using only one of many possible approaches, and we will explore several of them. Secondly, the jargon is completely unnecessary. The aim of this book is to avoid technical language wherever possible, and to explain technicalities in straightforward language where unavoidable. Your accountant and bank manager will use terms such as 'assets', 'net present value' and 'balance sheet' in a technical way. It will stand you in good stead to understand what is meant by these phrases, if only to find out whether they do too. But we must be clear in understanding the difference between knowing something, and merely knowing the name of something. Too many business people (and professionals) use shorthand to cover up a lack of detailed insight. Do not fear 'net present value' or any other phrases: they will be explained as we go along.

You may have noticed that I suggested that *when* you ask is important. The reason may not be obvious, but here is a stark example. I know of someone who had their business valued by an accountant at around £2 million, yet six months later the business was sold for £1 plus a load of debt. A year or so later it was wound up completely. Having a £2 million business turn into nothing more or less over night really does bring the phrase 'paper money' into sharp focus. How did this happen? Surely the accountant was incompetent and got the figure wildly wrong. Perhaps, but if I use the phrase 'dot com era' you may begin to understand how this could have happened. Remember how very many businesses were rapidly over-valued at this time? The stock market placed silly values on organizations that were haemorrhaging money, had few customers and unproven business models. The strange dot com phenomenon of the early years of this century proves the point that business valuations can be driven by emotion, rather than the logical application of reason. On the subject of the stock market, although this book is aimed at small businesses, lessons may be learnt from how the largest businesses are valued at the time of floatation (when shares are initially offered to the general public). Insights from these initial public offerings will be provided in Chapter 2. It may be enlightening and amusing to understand how real 'professionals' do it.

For now just note that *when* your business is valued may be as important as how it is valued – whether your run a dot com, guest house or budding plc. This point will be developed during the coming chapters.

A variety of approaches to valuing your business will be considered in Chapter 2, taking into account discussions with accountants, bank managers, business brokers and entrepreneurs. Having multiple approaches provides the best chance of achieving the most appropriate valuation, and should provide ideas for increasing the value others put on your business.

As Chapter 2 deals with approaches to *valuing* a business, the first chapter will examine *who will buy your business?* Why begin with this question? Well, whatever valuation model you use, the business will not be sold if you don't attract a buyer.

SELLING YOUR BUSINESS

If you already run a business, are in the process of launching a business, or are just considering starting a business, you need to think about selling it. If this appears to be a contradictory statement let me assure you that it isn't. Phrased differently, you need to consider *right now* how you will sell your business when the time comes. If you wait until you want to get out (or even worse, need to get out) it will probably be too late, and you may very well fail to realize the sale, or at least be forced to accept a low valuation. You cannot begin planning your exit too soon. Begin planning your departure now, even if it is years away.

There are 4.3 million enterprises in the United Kingdom and thousands are bought and sold each year. I know people who have made themselves very rich by selling their businesses and others who have made more modest amounts. There are also tax advantages that we will discuss later.

You may think that selling a business is a technical exercise, involving solicitors, accountants and business brokers. Of course this is one part of the process, but it is the relatively easy part. Any experienced and competent professional can help with this aspect, and we will consider how the technical part of the sale is managed in Chapters 4 and 6. Of much greater significance (and therefore covered in earlier chapters) are the things that you can do to maximize the selling price of your business, and how you can identify and attract people who would like to buy it.

Even if you run a modest business, say a hairdressing salon, corner shop or small plumbing firm, it is possible to develop its value into a very significant figure. Your business could become your most valuable asset – substantially more so than your home. Of course, some people run large and complex businesses and these can be sold for huge amounts. I know someone who runs a £30 million turnover business and is working to a three-year plan to sell it. The principles that he is following to maximize the sale value of his business are the same as you should follow – even though you may run a much more modest concern.

We live in a world of increasing entrepreneurship and if you already run a business you will be exhibiting the motivation and determination that are necessary to succeed. If you are in the early stages of developing your business you are probably brimming with enthusiasm and energy. For many people the most attractive feature of setting up a business is to 'go it alone'; to demonstrate to yourself and others that you can succeed in a challenging venture. It is not necessarily about making money – money is just one way of keeping count. Well, I hope you retain this attitude because you are going to need it. As your business develops you may begin to employ more people, have to make substantial capital investments, and become more involved in managing an organization (your own), and this can feel very different from the early stages when you experience the joys of working for yourself. In my case, when I reached the point where most of my time was spent managing others, my enthusiasm waned somewhat and I began to feel like an employee again. Will this happen to you? Has it already happened? Who knows? But my advice is to invest time and resources now to ensure that if there comes a time when you are losing enthusiasm for your business you are able to make a profitable exit. You don't want to end up locked into a burdensome routine where you are nominally in charge but in reality have few options other than to keep working 50 or 60 hours a week. Of course, some people are able to maintain interest in a business for decades, but don't assume that this will be the case for you. Even hyper-motivated people like Sir Richard Branson need to maintain enthusiasm by setting up new ventures and selling old ones.

REAL-LIFE CASE STUDIES

Business books can be a little dry, but the people behind businesses rarely are. This book will explore a number of short case studies based on people who have successfully been through the process of selling a business. One such person is Tony Gill, who has disposed of two businesses, made himself rich and has picked up the UK National Entrepreneur of the Year award along the way. Tony's story will be unveiled in small chunks as the book progresses. It may be interesting to briefly consider the background to his business career before moving on.

The serial entrepreneur

Tony Gill started his first business whilst in his early 20s and was a multi-millionaire with a significant business sale behind him by his early 30s. In 2002, having achieved even greater success, he won the UK National Entrepreneur of the Year award. Now in his early 40s he has completed yet another substantial business sale and retains a commercial interest in a number of small but rapidly developing businesses.

Whilst his level of achievement goes far beyond the norm, his is a typical story of the working-class lad who under-achieved at school and left at the first opportunity, but went on to excel in the world of business. This book will focus on the kind of attitude and approaches that led him through two very significant business disposals. However, it may be enlightening to consider the factors behind his approach to business, which will help make sense of his success in selling his businesses at the most opportune time.

Tony doesn't call himself a businessman. His preferred word is 'entrepreneur', the definition of which is difficult to tie down. Of course, 'risk' is inherent in the mind of the entrepreneur, but for Tony it goes further. He suggests that true entrepreneurs are prepared to risk 'self-destruction'. I guess he means by this having the mindset to gamble everything you have on your own talent and ability to deliver. (Someone suggested to me that another feature of the entrepreneurial psyche involves 'having no concept of work–life balance'!)

Anyone who has read Richards Branson's books will have noted that at various points in his career Branson was prepared to back himself 100 per cent even when failure would have been catastrophic on a personal level. And it is obvious why the average corporate executive does not have this mindset. If you have been appointed CEO of a large public company it is probably more important to manage 'the downside' than to take significant risks in developing the business. And I believe there is another key difference. Entrepreneurs are creators. They take very little and turn it into a lot, whereas your average senior executive is a manager who takes significant assets and develops them modestly through time. If they do a little better than the rest of the market they become heroes in the business pages and make a fortune in profit-related bonuses. Even so, they should not confuse themselves with entrepreneurs.

Are entrepreneurs born or do they develop? Who knows, but in Tony's case being advised by a teacher that he 'wouldn't even find a job' seemed to act as a spur. Immediately he landed his first role he was happy to be first in at work in the morning, would volunteer for any task, and considered the whole process to be one of 'learning on the job'. By 19 years of age he had been poached by rival firms several times and was eventually backed by a larger firm to open a new branch in Leeds. The Leeds business grew successfully but the parent company over-stretched its assets and went into receivership. The process led to Tony's home being sold to pay his personal liability against bank guarantees. This experience of being part of a failure appears to have scarred Tony but also taught him valuable lessons. With about £30,000 that was leftover from the house sale, he and his wife founded their own business. Having such a low capital base meant they had to be careful with both cash and credit. They managed cash flow tightly, were very selective about offering extended payment terms and ran the business with 'good financial values'. In the first year they turned a very modest profit. Over the next five years both revenue and profit increased significantly. All profits were reinvested in the business and they had a modest lifestyle, taking relatively low salaries and driving inexpensive cars. By their seventh year in business, turnover reached about £8 million and significant profits were being generated.

As all entrepreneurs know, growing a business is a much more difficult task than is suggested by the few brief sentences above. There are many challenges, and big decisions that have to be faced. At one stage Tony wanted to make a very major investment in machinery that would broaden the operation of the business and could pave the way to higher profits. The investment was not without risk and Tony failed to convince his wife (and business partner) that they should use all the capital that had been accumulated by the business – and borrow significantly from the bank – to fund the machinery purchase. They had an informal arrangement with their accountant that, at times when the husband and wife team could not agree on a business issue, they would use him as a 'third head' – a kind of referee. This is probably a common arrangement in all types of businesses that have two partners or directors. On hearing Tony's plans the accountant supported Tony's wife's view that the investment was too big a step at this time. An aggrieved Tony pushed the accountant for a full explanation which, when forthcoming, was along the lines of 'You have grown a successful and profitable business over a number of years. Why risk it all on the back of one big investment?' Perhaps this is an example of the 'self-destruct' approach that Tony believes is the lot of the true entrepreneur. 'Why risk everything? Because I need to.' Eventually all parties became convinced that the investment represented a good (if risky) opportunity and the new machinery was duly purchased. The business went on to greater success.

After about eight years the partners decided it was time to cash in. They had continued to live relatively modestly and had reinvested almost all profits back into the business, which now represented a very large (yet in hard cash terms theoretical) asset. How was a buyer found? How was the business valued? These questions will be answered in Chapters 1 and 2. The structure of the book, and how it relates to the big questions such as these, is detailed below.

STRUCTURE OF THIS BOOK

The first question to be posed is 'Who will buy your business?' This is a good question and a sensible place to start. Sometimes the answer is not obvious. But there are many things you can do to get your business noticed by people who would want to buy it and this will be explored in detail in the first chapter.

As previously mentioned, Chapter 2 takes an in-depth look at different models for valuing a business. It also considers approaches aimed at maximizing value. There are many activities that can help increase how much others will be prepared to pay.

Chapter 3 considers how to exit your business. This could be as simple as someone handing over a large cheque and you popping down to the bank to cash it, whilst heading for your new home in the Bahamas. Often, however, the process for managing yourself out of a business that you have personally grown and developed can be complicated, and if you are not careful could take years. Developing an exit strategy is as important as planning for retirement.

Chapter 4 will focus on how to handle accountants, solicitors and transfer agents. If you are not careful their fees can seriously erode your profit. However, good professional advisers who are well managed can add immeasurable value. Within this chapter we will address questions such as 'How should I select an accountant or solicitor?' 'Should I engage a business broker?' 'How can my bank manager help?' 'How far ahead of the sale do I require professional advice?'

In Chapter 5, low-cost ways to get your business noticed are explored – a kind of DIY public relations approach. With a little careful thought any business can generate publicity. Having a couple of articles published in the relevant trade press helped develop the interest that ultimately led to the sale of my business. Of course, you have to ensure that you are giving the most effective message to the right people.

Chapters 6 to 9 concentrate on how to manage the sale process and also the post-sale period, when you may have to remain involved in the business for a time. Although you should not expect the whole process to progress smoothly, there are many things you can do to ensure that things stay on track. Most importantly, you need to remain in control. Many of the lessons in these chapters are based on things that I and others did not get right. Sometimes the strongest learning happens when we mess up. Chapter 8 includes advice for specific business sectors such as retailers, consultants and manufacturers.

Chapter 10 takes a look at what others have done with their time following the successful sale of a business. Its objective is to inspire you. After all, dreams may be what keep you motivated through the difficult years of running – and then selling – your business. Will you follow in the footsteps of the 60-year old who signed up for a Sports Science degree, or run for parliament? The key thing about successfully selling a business is that it gives you choices, and the time to make them, even if you have only had a relatively modest success.

The final chapter is short but important. In addition to good planning and clear thinking, selling a business requires action. This chapter pulls together a number of activities with the objective of encouraging you to begin the process of planning ahead.

Before moving on it should be noted that throughout the book reference is made to 'selling the shares in a business'. Many businesses are obviously 'incorporated', which means they are formal limited liability companies that have shareholders. However, many people operate businesses that take other legal forms, sole traders or partnerships being the most common. If you are a sole trader or work in partnership you will not be selling the shares in your business because it doesn't have any. You will be selling its assets, along with goodwill. Most of the details in this book are relevant whether you run a limited company or operate under some other legal format. However, there are occasions when the legal structure of your business will be very important and you should take early professional advice.

Let us now explore the first major question. Who will buy your business?

1

Who Will Buy Your Business?

Selling a business involves harnessing the passion that allowed you to begin and then grow your business to the process of successfully selling it. This means being positive, motivated and *active*. You *can* sell your business. Thousands of businesses are bought and sold each year. Some acquisitions are of national importance involving eye-watering sums and occasionally make a headline on the evening news, especially if the owner has a beard and continually attempts hot air balloon trips around the world. Other deals receive zero publicity, except perhaps the noticeable appearance of a new face behind the Post Office counter, or an 'under new management banner' tied to the shopfront. Open your eyes and ears. You will uncover a great deal of evidence indicating that businesses are continually bought and sold.

For someone to buy your business they first have to be aware of its existence. Not really an earth-shattering observation, but an important one. In the broadest terms there are two ways that people will know of your business. The first is that the prospective purchaser has some existing relationship with you, perhaps as a competitor, supplier, customer or employee. Depending on your business sector, these relationships can provide excellent opportunities for a profitable sale. I sold my business to a much larger competitor after successfully winning a major customer from them. They wondered how a small business with a very short pedigree could steal a major account and became interested to find out more about us. The second way that people will become aware of your existence is by engaging in marketing activities, either undertaken by yourself directly, or perhaps using a marketing organization or business broker to act on your behalf. Chapter 5 deals with this very important topic, so for now I will concentrate on how to take advantage of the existing relationships that your business inevitably has.

COMPETITORS

Competitors may have many reasons for wishing to buy your business. For example, if you run a hairdressing salon a local competitor may be attracted to your business because:

I you have the prime location in town and the only way to take it is to buy your business as a going concern;
I you have an impressive customer base that they are having difficulty in taking from you by competitive means;
I buying your business would reduce competition and allow them to push up prices;
I your staff are excellent, loyal and hard to poach;
I others calculate that a quick return on investment is possible – believing that they could make more money from your business than you do;
I they want to grow quickly (many entrepreneurs seek rapid expansion, often at the expense of profitability, cash flow and common sense).

Of course the above is not unique to hairdressing businesses. Consider retailers. Many retailers buy competitors for one or more of the reasons noted above – even the major national chains. Your local Morrison's supermarket may well have been a Safeway store just a few years ago. The fact that the Safeway acquisition was a large national deal makes no difference to the principles. All retailers compete on a local basis and buying competitors is one of the few ways that market share can be quickly increased and competition diminished. And it's not just retailers. I know a very successful company that sells photocopiers and office equipment (it would tell you that it provides 'communications solutions', but it really sells photocopiers and other printing devices). It has a turnover of over £100 million per annum and part of its growth strategy is to buy small local competitors throughout the United Kingdom. Most years it makes several acquisitions, with the result that an increasing number of local business people now have extremely healthy bank accounts, and a golden glow that suggests a great deal of time spent on a Spanish golf course.

Think about it. Setting up a new business (or branch) in another town is a major undertaking that takes time and is full of risk. Premises, staff, customers and a supply infrastructure are required. Acquiring these elements can be costly, difficult and time-consuming. When buying an established business most of the hassle has been taken care of – and it is logical that a premium should be paid. The challenge for you is to ensure that if you sell out to a competitor the premium is maximized to your advantage.

Activity: List your competitors

Make a list of all of your competitors. Why would they be interested in buying your business? Write down all the reasons that occur to you.

Keep this list and reflect on it as you progress through the rest of this book. Add to the list as further ideas emerge.

Should you decide that selling your business to a competitor is a realistic prospect, you have two choices. The most direct involves calling them and asking 'Do you want to buy me out?' If this sounds like a slightly unlikely route to a successful sale, think again. Our serial entrepreneur did just that when he decided to sell his first business.

The serial entrepreneur

In the Introduction, Tony Gill's story was left at a point where he had grown a profitable business over eight years and decided it was time to cash in – in an attempt to secure the financial future of his family. His lack of experience in selling a business did not deter Tony from taking a very direct approach. Having 'researched' competitors through trade magazines (the internet was not very well developed in those days) he created a list of companies that he thought might have the funds, and inclination, to acquire his business. This is an effective method of research. Many large and acquisitive companies like to publicize purchases either for egotistical or good business reasons. The first company contacted was interested in discussing things further and its managing director arrived the following day to begin talks. Nine months later a profitable sale was concluded.

Tony's approach was slightly more subtle than might be suggested by the above description. His opening conversation with the potential buyer was on the lines of 'I have a good business and it could be even more successful if it was part of a group.' You can imagine that this kind of opening might be a little more intriguing to the recipient than the more direct 'Well, do you want to buy my business or not?'

Perhaps there are reasons that a direct approach would not be appropriate for you. Before examining a slightly gentler approach it is worth taking a moment to think about timescales, which will be an important consideration for many later chapters. If you bought this book because you are desperate to sell your business very quickly, options will be restricted. You will need to adopt direct routes to getting things done. To take the current example, making a list of all competitors and then contacting them for a 'how about it' conversation may actually be a reasonable strategy. However, if you are planning ahead to a time when several competitors may bid to buy your business, the subtle approach might feel like a more acceptable strategy. Whatever the case, the maxim 'If you don't ask, you don't get' is directly applicable to the challenge of achieving a profitable sale.

Like most business activities, developing a formal strategy of being noticed by competitors involves both opportunities and risks, the specific blend of which depends on your unique circumstances. On the positive side, perhaps the most logical way of drawing attention to your business is by a continuous process of winning new customers. In almost all situations this will be achieved at the expense of competitors. This is what your business should be doing anyway, so where is the downside? Well, the key question revolves around how your competitors will respond. They could respond by pulling out a cheque book and pleading with you to sell your business to them. On the other hand, they could become offensive and attempt a local price war or some other form of predatory action. A recent report on national radio suggested that two major national food retailers have local predatory pricing campaigns with the objective of putting successful local competitors out of business. The supermarkets denied the allegation, but this does not necessarily mean they are innocent. On balance you might favour being brave, as competitors (in the guise of potential buyers) may be too big a sale prospect to ignore. If the competition has never heard of you, then no one else will have either, so stop hiding your light under a bushel (or in the warehouse) and get noticed.

Some organizations view their competitors as enemies, with the result that no communication exists between the different businesses. Well, mine may be a contrary view but I don't think it has to be like this. You have something in common with your competitors – how you earn a living. By logical extension you will know a lot of the same suppliers and customers. Why not take every opportunity to meet and talk to them? Perhaps this could be at local events, such as Chamber of Commerce dinners. A competitor who knows you (more important, trusts you) is infinitely more likely to show an interest in your business. Cultivate the competition.

SUPPLIERS

Business generates some fantastic jargon, and I have made a promise to myself to avoid it at all costs. Occasionally it will be necessary to break the rule. Many years ago someone coined the phrase 'vertical integration'. For the uninitiated 'vertical integration' relates to the idea that businesses can be more efficient (or make more money) if they own more and more of the processes between raw materials and the final product being delivered to the customer. In formal business-speak, this is 'vertical integration within the supply chain'.

Large brewers are a good example of this phenomenon in action. First of all they take hops, barley, sugar and water, boil them up and produce a miraculous liquid called beer. Having done this they have a wide range of opportunities for vertically integrating their business to a point much closer to final customers enjoying a pint in the pub. The most obvious and successful way of achieving this involves owning the pub as well. That way they can ensure that all beer sold in the pub is their own (or products supplied by official partners), and they get to take the retail profit in addition to the wholesale profit. Large brewers developed such enthusiasm for this activity that eventually the Department of Trade and Industry had to intervene and tell them to stop. Some organizations were forced to sell hundreds of public houses because they had negatively affected all of the competition in certain regions. Vertical integration may be good for business but it is not always in the best interest of consumers.

If you own a successful pub there is a reasonable prospect that a brewery would be interested in buying it. Then they will vertically integrate their beer into your cellar. But it is not only brewers. Perhaps you have a small local double-glazing business. The company that supplies your extruded PVC may well be interested in taking over your business. It can then join the brewers in their enjoyment of wholesale and retail profits.

Does vertical integration make sense in your business sector? It depends, but a little logical thought should suggest a clear answer. If you own a newspaper shop it is unlikely that Mirror Group Newspapers will want to buy you out. Why? Isn't the scenario similar to that of the brewers? Similar yes, but the difference lies with product exclusivity. If Mirror Group buys your shop and just sells its own newspapers, everyone who reads *The Sun, The Times* and all other non-MGN papers is going to shop elsewhere.

Please don't get the impression that this kind of activity is limited to large companies. In many areas small local farmers have taken to converting a barn into a farm shop. This is vertical integration in action. Farmers become retailers, and if they prepare vegetables into home-made soup before selling them in the small café at the side of the shop they have integrated into being restaurateurs. It is all about adding value and increasing profits. The key point to focus on is that your business could provide a method for people further down the supply chain (more jargon, sorry) to get closer to the final customer. Having cultivated your competitors, you should also serenade your suppliers.

Activity: List your suppliers

Make a list of all of your major suppliers. Why would they be interested in buying your business? As with the earlier activity, write down all the reasons that occur to you.

Keep this list and reflect on it as you progress through the rest of this book. Add to the list as further ideas emerge.

CUSTOMERS

Why might a customer be interested in buying your business? The obvious reason is that it already buys your products or services, and therefore has an existing requirement for them (or at the very least an interest). The level of interest will be significantly affected by the type of business you operate. If you are in a sector where vertical integration makes sense, it may have occurred to you that your customers are just one step ahead of you in the supply chain, and may well see benefits in integrating backwards. It has been known for pub chains to buy small local brewing companies. Why? They may get exclusive rights to the product and the potential for increased profits.

For the purposes of this book I consider that any business that sells directly to the public and where the transaction is made on the business's premises is a *retailer*. This definition obviously includes shops, hotels, pubs, garages and many other service- or product-based businesses. You may think the definition is so broad as to be effectively arbitrary, but there is some logic in the approach. Aside from selling directly to the general public, all of these businesses share common characteristics. For example, location will be important, as will the need to make regular repeat sales. Most will have very many customers who make relatively small purchases. The majority of customers will obviously have no interest in buying your business. But some might – you only need one person who has both the motivation and assets, so don't ignore your customer base.

One of the ways of adding serious value to your business is to know who your customers are, what they buy and where they live. Have you ever wondered why large retailers go to the trouble of introducing loyalty cards? It's certainly not just loyalty. When you use the card they get a record of what you bought, when and how much you spent. They can also determine whether you own a pet or suffer with dandruff. They can see what you buy and this tells them a lot about who you are. Even though you may operate on a much smaller scale, the more you know about customers the better, and the value of doing so will be explored in detail in Chapter 2. For now, just remember the nauseating television advertisement from the 1980s where the man was so impressed with the shaver he bought the company. Perhaps Magners Irish Cider will be so impressed with your apples that it buys the orchard. Then you really will have 'time dedicated to you'.

Activity: List your customers

Make a list of all of your major customers. Why would they be interested in buying your business? As with the earlier activities, write down all the reasons that occur to you.

Keep this list and reflect on it as you progress through the rest of this book. Add to the list as further ideas emerge.

EMPLOYEES

Employees frequently buy out existing owners. For once the business-speak jargon is both apt and accurate: the management buyout (MBO). Many firms, both large and small, have changed hands in this way. The MBO has many attractive features. The team buying the company already know customers, suppliers and other staff. Good for continuity. Also the buyer and seller know each other, so hopefully an element of trust and goodwill will permeate the sale process. From the seller's side there may also be some satisfaction in seeing the business they have grown and nurtured continuing to thrive.

Despite these advantages, a business bank manager I recently spoke to advised that his bank was often sceptical about lending money to employees involved in MBOs. It is not that they won't lend the money, but they will be cautious. Why are banks cautious about lending money in MBO situations? They must have seen many businesses fail. Why do MBOs fail? Probably for a number of reasons, but one demands particular attention. Money borrowed from the bank has to be paid back with interest. Remember the loan did not exist before the MBO. It is a new burden on profitability. Can the new management team increase profitability? Obviously sometimes they can, but my bank manager friend indicates that post-MBO profits are often over-estimated, with the result that the business under new management struggles to survive.

Would you care if this happened? Obviously it would be nice to hear about the continued success of your business when your management team has taken over, but a financial reason could also exist. Perhaps part of the sale fee will be paid out of future profits, which I have already suggested will have to increase to cover loan interest and capital repayment. Ideas for ensuring you get all money owed are dealt with in Chapter 3. For now let us briefly examine a short real-world example that considers how your employees can be encouraged to succeed when you step out of the business.

The joinery business (part 1)

Martin ran a small joinery business for 10 years. He employed 10 joiners, a foreman and an all-round assistant who would liaise with suppliers and assist in other general office work. Martin was the key contact for all customers, managed the finances and took all major decisions. The business would struggle to function properly if Martin was away for more than a couple of weeks.

Deciding to take early retirement, Martin reflected on the best strategy for exiting his business. He was keen to reward his office assistant and foreman by allowing them to buy the business from him at a very fair price. But he was concerned about their lack of commercial experience, and ability to raise finance. He didn't want to have a drawn out arrangement where he was paid out of profits because, as he remarked, 'At the moment all profit is mine, so I would be buying the business with my own money.' A wise observation.

His solution was to approach an acquaintance who already ran a business, with the idea that he jointly buy the joinery business along with the two existing employees already mentioned. The outsider would bring commercial skills and cash, whilst the current employees would provide knowledge of how the business operated, and continuity. A simple but elegant solution that worked well. However, whilst Martin successfully sold his business and secured a cash payment, the price he received was nothing like what he should have achieved. He practically gave away a very profitable business. I will return to the story in Chapter 2 to consider how Martin could have achieved a much more profitable result, whilst treating his employees equitably.

FRANCHISE BUSINESSES

Operating a franchise can be a very successful model for running a profitable business, but can lead to difficulties (and also opportunities) when the time comes to sell. The first activity you should undertake is to check what your franchise agreement says about disposal. It could be that disposal is not referred to in the agreement, and you are therefore free to sell to whomever and however you wish. However, for some service-based franchises there may be uncertainty about who 'owns' the clients and therefore which party is entitled to financially benefit from the goodwill generated. It may be, for example, that certain national clients are ring-fenced and excluded from the turnover of your business. It could also be that you are merely an 'agent' of the wider business, and whilst entitled to profits generated by your specific activities, will not be in a position to sell the business for a capital sum. Another potential issue is that the franchisor may wish to impose rules to the extent that potential purchasers may have to meet certain requirements. It could be, for example, that they are required to have a certain amount of working capital, or need specific qualifications. It may also be that the franchising organization can help you to sell your business. First, it may make capital available to prospective purchasers, and secondly might actually help you find a buyer. It could be it has other franchisees who would wish to expand into your geographic region.

Check your agreement now to determine the rules surrounding how you can exit the franchise.

PRIVATE EQUITY FIRMS

There are a number of specialist organizations that invest in private businesses by buying equity – another term for buying shares. They are usually known as either 'private equity investors' or 'venture capitalists'. Generally their objective is to put money into a business to allow it to expand and develop, with a view to making a profitable exit in around three to five years' time. It follows that they are looking to identify businesses with strong management teams that can deliver significant profitable growth in a relative short time period. Given that you are looking to exit the business, you would need to ensure that you were leaving behind a strong team capable of such delivery – using a private equity firm could therefore be an option if you are considering some form of MBO where employees take only part of the shares. Usually, private equity investors are looking to buy into firms of a reasonable size rather than very small businesses. However, you should raise the issue with your accountant, who may be able to advise whether your business may be attractive to private equity investors.

BUSINESS ANGELS

The term 'business angels' has become quite commonplace in recent years. In the region where I live there is a thriving business angels community. Basically, business angels are people with spare capital (and often business experience) who are interested in finding opportunities to invest in small firms that require additional capital and may also benefit from their expertise. Many business angels have owned and then disposed of their own businesses – perhaps you might become one yourself. As with private equity firms, business angels are not usually interested in becoming owner-managers. They don't want to run the business, merely offer financial investment and perhaps mentoring of the management team. Business angels may therefore be appropriate where an MBO is potentially the best disposal route. Often business angels are able to bridge any funding gaps that occur during an MBO process. For example, perhaps your management team does not have enough equity in their homes (or other private assets) that would allow a bank to lend them the full amount required to buy your business. A business angel might be prepared to provide capital to cover the difference, in return for an equity stake in the business. (A contact address for the national business angels organization is provided in Appendix B.)

Much of this chapter has focused on how people who are already aware of your business may be interested in acquiring it. Obviously, limiting potential buyers to people you know is quite a large restriction. How can broader interest be generated? This forms the core of Chapter 5 – 'Marketing Your Business'.

Chapter summary

▮ Successfully selling a business requires you to be positive, motivated and active – the very qualities that enabled you to develop your business.

▮ People who know of your business may be interested in buying it. This may include competitors, suppliers and customers.

▮ Management buyouts are quite common. Just because your management team do not have the personal wealth to buy the business does not mean they can't do so. Funding may be made available by banks, private equity investors, business angels or other sources of finance.

▮ Taking a direct approach may be effective – especially if you want to make a quick exit. Remember how the serial entrepreneur researched competitors and then picked up the telephone.

2

Valuing Your Business

'There are not two certainties in life but three. Death, taxes and *the valuation is wrong.*' This pithy but apt advice was given to me by an experienced accountant. He went on to produce even more interesting observations: 'When it comes to business valuations somebody – the buyer or the seller – is always wrong. Sometimes they both are. The perfect price does not exist.' I include these observations not to depress you, but to encourage you to realize that calculating the value of your business is an art form, not a strict science. Business valuations are not measured using compasses, thermometers, pedometers, rev-counters or any other type of empirical tool; they are measured by human emotion, (hopefully) supported by a range of hard data and rules of thumb. Turning the question around, I asked my accountant friend what the buyer was paying for when acquiring a business. 'Hope', he advised.

A little cynical? Perhaps, but I prefer to see these observations as the views of an experienced and qualified commentator. As such we should bear them in mind when we consider the more positive factors that make up the remainder of this chapter.

SELL MORE, CHARGE MORE, SPEND LESS

There are three things that a business can do to increase profits: sell more, charge more and spend less. Just about any activity you can name that will improve profitability can be traced back to one or more of these activities. It is not surprising therefore that these factors will be in the mind of the prospective purchaser. If they believe that it would be possible to sell more than your business currently achieves, or maybe to charge a higher price for the products you supply (perhaps by repackaging or moving upmarket), they will feel able to justify paying more for your business. This leads me on to one of my least favourite of all 'business-speak' terms: 'synergy'. How often have you read in the newspaper that firm X has bought company Y for £Z million and is confident that 'synergies' between the two companies will deliver an impressive payback? The idea is that these synergies can help the firm to:

▮ *Sell more*: perhaps an events management business decides to move into 'in-house catering'. Acquiring a catering business could create opportunities for selling many more hot-dogs, drinks and snacks, with a resulting increase in profit.
▮ *Charge more*: the events business now has its own catering division and no longer allows competitor hot-dog sellers or other food vendors on site. In these circumstances (a captive audience and zero competition) it would not be difficult to increase prices.
▮ *Spend less*: the events business makes all of the overhead staff in the acquired catering business redundant as it only requires one finance, marketing and HR team.

Ensure that you factor opportunities for achieving 'synergies' into your valuation – whatever methods you decide to employ.

Activity: Look for synergies

Consider your business but try to do so from an outsider's perspective. What opportunities for synergies might be present? Under what conditions could they sell, charge more or spend less? For example, would a larger business be able to bid for larger contracts? Or reduce overheads? Or take advantage of leveraging lower prices from suppliers?

A LITTLE ECONOMIC PHILOSOPHY

I promised in the introductory chapter that this book aims to be practical and genuinely useful. At the risk of stretching this commitment I now want to spend a little time considering changes in the broader economy that influence the value attributed to specific types of business. In doing so I will use practical examples in an attempt to avoid becoming a woolly commentator. Hopefully the importance of this section will quickly become clear to you.

Not too long ago businesses generally required capital to make things. Available finance was mixed with raw materials and human labour and a whole world full of products were wrought into being. However, in modern developed economies there has been a major shift towards other factors of 'production' which, although similar to historical elements, combine to add large amounts of value in strange and interesting ways. In essence those of us who are fortunate enough to live in advanced economies live in an environment that is driven by knowledge. Competitive advantage is now often found in data, design, creativity and in harnessing innovative ways of exploiting information, rather than building bigger factories or storing up ever greater amounts of capital. Branding and know-how are increasingly becoming the most significant way of adding value for both customers and shareholders. In summary, the most valuable modern-day assets are to be found in our heads rather than our factories. Taking a little time to explore what is in your head may result in your business developing into a much more valuable entity, although just because ideas can add value doesn't mean they will. Ideas can be inappropriate, silly or just plain wrong. However, the best ideas can add significant value to a business. Let me provide a practical example from a sector I have a little experience in.

The printing industry

The printing industry is diverse, has a long history and is an important business sector (in so much as its products are touched and used by millions of people in all walks of life). Producers of print include newspaper, book and magazine publishers, businesses large and small and almost all parts of the public sector. The aspect I wish to focus on (by way of example) is the commercial print sector. This includes printers who publish brochures, stationery, forms, envelopes, mailings and other materials that enable their customers to communicate – in turn – with customers further up the supply chain.

The amount of printed material produced on behalf of businesses has grown significantly over recent decades. The professionalization of marketing activities has lead to an ever increasing volume of printed materials being utilized. To experience the results of this phenomenon step into any high street bank and you will see many examples of expensively printed materials enticing you to buy a whole range of financial products. You will also find printed banners hanging from the ceiling and printed posters adorning the windows. Printed materials are all around us (you probably have some in your wallet or purse – even your credit card is printed).

To meet the increasing demand for printed products the industry has grown in size and radically increased productivity. Machines used in the print process are now faster and more efficient that ever, and equipment is becoming increasingly sophisticated and expensive. Does this sound like a good sector to be involved in? You might think so, but the problem is that as demand has grown so has the number of entrants into the print market, to the extent that many people suggest a significant over-capacity has existed for many years. Many printing firms have responded to this challenge by investing in ever more expensive equipment on the grounds that this will enable them to produce materials quicker and cheaper than competitors, thus providing competitive advantage. One unfortunate downside of this approach is that quicker machines push up capacity and need ever increasing amounts of business to feed the equipment and also to pay for it. A spiral of increasing difficulty ensues. Being a profitable and successful commercial printer is tough, although, as in all areas of economic life, some firms are more successful than others.

One of the tactics that businesses employ when faced with challenging market conditions is to acquire other businesses, or arrange mergers or invest in even faster and more efficient equipment. You might expect that this is the model that is generating most success within the print industry? It may work for some, but many of the most successful printing organizations in recent years (in terms of profits, revenue growth and shareholder value) have arisen out of a very different approach. The most successful firms in the sector have used knowledge and information technology, rather than efficient productive technology. In short, they have innovated in a way that delivers value for both customers and shareholders, and many of the most lucrative business disposals in the industry have involved firms that use the knowledge-based model. What I am describing is the rise of the 'print management' company.

Print management doesn't sound like a radical (or indeed sexy) term because it isn't. But the difference between a print manufacturer and a print manager is very significant. One has to invest large amounts of capital in equipment, employ lots of expensive production labour and find customers who will provide a consistent stream of work in a very competitive market. The other simply has to understand what customers need and find a cost-effective solution for providing it; without the factory, warehouse or expensive production staff.

The print management company does two things. First, it invests time in understanding the complex demands of large customers (think about the high street bank example – it produces thousands of different print products each year and is constantly innovating in terms of design, materials and so on). It may be necessary for the print manager to create bespoke IT software to help identify and manage shifting requirements, and this is an excellent way of locking customers in. If customers use the print manager's software, it will be difficult to replace as a suppler.

The second thing print managers do is use the over-capacity in the market to drive down prices. They buy on behalf of customers from whichever manufacturers currently offer the lowest prices. This enables them to offer excellent value to customers whilst making an attractive margin for themselves. And here is the really interesting part from our current perspective. Because they 'own' the customer relationship (and lock customers into medium- or long-term contracts), the sale value of their businesses can be staggeringly high. Over the last couple of years the biggest business disposals and acquisitions in the sector have involved print management organizations.

So print management involves knowledge, ideas and creativity, in an industry that used to rely on large amounts of capital and huge workforces. It exemplifies the shift from machines and raw materials to data and relationships, and the market value of the businesses concerned reflects the success of the approach. A word of warning. Before you rush off to sell your business and launch a new print management company be advised that the market is getting pretty crowded, and it may be that the golden era has passed. The real point is to encourage you to think more laterally about your own business, and the sector that you operate in. It is just possible that thinking in terms of knowledge, ideas, relationships, creativity – whatever – may enable you to add significant value to your business in a modest timescale. It's about finding the recipe for increasing value. Unfortunately, I can't tell you exactly what your businesses recipe might be. I really wish I could.

Back to the mundane matter of valuing a business. Before examining a variety of tools and approaches that may help us to successfully do so, it is worth reflecting on broader and bigger issues. The following factors may influence the valuation of a business, whatever method is used. In other words, it considers the elements that will be important to potential buyers.

CUSTOMER BASE

The nature of your customer base will have a significant impact on how others value your business. Your business may be successful and profitable, but if it depends on only one or two customers for most of its revenue, a potential buyer is going to consider this a significant risk, unless of course you have some form of long-term agreement that locks in the customer. In the last chapter we read about a joinery business that was successfully sold to a combination of two employees plus an external investor. The value of that particular business would have been several times greater had the spread of customers been broader.

The joinery business (part 2)

Martin's joinery business relied on one very large retail customer for about 90 per cent of its revenue. Martin's relationship with the customer was good and he knew many of the key people in the organization socially, as well as having a business relationship. Knowing when he was onto a good thing, Martin looked after his single customer very well, always meeting tight deadlines and providing high-quality products. The customer stayed loyal over a period of 10 years, and although expenditure fluctuated somewhat, Martin could always rely on it covering a very high proportion of his turnover. This relationship was so successful that Martin never needed to market his business or find other customers, as he had no desire to grow the business beyond the size where he could manage all aspects himself. Occasionally work would be completed for other customers, but this involved responding to requests rather than actively generating new sources of business. A successful strategy? Certainly, until the time came to sell the business, whereupon the single customer became a real issue in terms of sale value.

Let us imagine that Martin's firm had 20 more or less equal customers, rather than the solitary one that he relied on. It is not unreasonable to suppose that the business might be valued at say five to eight times the value of post-tax profits. Instead, having one customer meant that he actually sold the business for less than the value of one year's post-tax profits – a very significant difference.

Martin's strategy was never to rely on growing the value of the business, and he was happy to discount the sale price to reward two existing employees when the time came to exit. Nevertheless, the story does identify the importance of considering the spread of customers when thinking about the value of a business.

In addition to the quantity of customers, *quality* is also important. For example, if you have a 'blue chip' client base that includes industry leaders, it may be possible to achieve a higher valuation. This may of course vary quite significantly between industry sectors.

PREDICTABILITY OF WORKLOAD

In general terms there are two things that influence how predictable demand for a business's services or products will be: having a broad spread of customers and having contracted revenue streams. Some firms (such as mobile phone companies) work hard to acquire both. The importance of the customer base was considered in the joinery case study above. However, contracted income can also be extremely important in influencing the value of a business. The reason will probably be obvious to you. If your firm is profitable this year and contracted income more or less guarantees that the business will at least maintain profitability for future years, the figures can be added together and, with a little clever accountancy, the net present value of this revenue can be predicted. ('Net present value' is explained below.)

COSTS UNDER CONTROL

If having a predictable volume of work is important, then controlling costs is also vital. Effectively this is the other side of the coin to generating revenue. Are the costs of operating your business predictable? Are they minimized? Do you suffer as a result of external factors that make your business susceptible to fluctuating costs? Does your business have a high proportion of fixed costs? Would it be possible for a potential buyer to lower the cost base by leveraging 'synergies' with their existing business or some similar method? Costs share equal importance with revenue when it comes to determining profitability, so ensure you understand how this relationship may affect the sale value of your business. In fact, reducing costs can often lead to faster and more substantial profit increases than growing sales. Take the following example.

Activity: Cutting costs

Imagine a business that has an annual turnover of £500,000. Let us assume it is a metal fabrication manufacturing business. Its (simplified) cost base is as follows:

Bought in goods and services: £230,000
Labour and related costs: £200,000
Profit: £70,000

Let us assume that by rigorous negotiations with steel suppliers, electricity companies and the third-party distribution company that they outsource deliveries to, annual savings of £23,000 are achieved. That's a 10 per cent reduction in bought in goods and services. However, this cost reduction actually increases profit from £70,000 to £93,000 – a 33 per cent increase. In this example, buying 10 per cent better increases profits by about a third.

Now let us consider increasing revenue. If the same business did not cut costs but decided to grow profits by increasing revenue, it may have to sell about £150,000 of additional business to achieve the same result. Sometimes cost control is overlooked – and not just in small companies.

Consider your business. What would be the effect on profit of a 10 per cent reduction in bought in goods and services? If you take this figure and multiply it by five (for the time being) you may get an indication of how much might be added to the sale price of your business. More on this later in the chapter.

MANAGEMENT

Does your business have a strong, stable management team or does it rely on you to make all key decisions? Will your team be happy to work under a new owner or will there be a threat of key personnel departing? The issue of your being 'locked-in' to the business for an extended period after the sale is dealt with later. For the moment you need to realize that the strength and capabilities within your team may be an important factor in how others value your business.

SUSTAINABLE PROFITS

The factors noted above – predictable workload, cost control and strong management – are all really components in delivering sustainable profits. The more sustainable profits are considered to be, the higher the sale value. Any potential purchaser will look at historical profit figures – over a period of at least three years – to help determine an accurate assessment. Of course, as all adverts for financial products are obliged to indicate, 'past performance is not an indication of future performance'. This is why all of the factors that support sustainable profits will attract significant attention from prospective buyers.

ASSETS

One simplistic method of valuing a business is to add up all of its assets and take away all liabilities. We look in more detail at the asset valuation model later in this chapter. For most businesses, focusing on the tangible assets will not be the most appropriate way of reaching a valuation. Some businesses have hardly any physical assets, yet have a high value based upon their ability to generate sustainable profits. However, for a limited range of businesses, for example a property business, assets may represent a very great deal of value, over and above the profits being generated. If your business falls into this category, ensure you take detailed advice from an accountant before considering the most appropriate valuation method.

STRATEGIC FIT

Your business may be of significant interest to a potential purchaser simply because it has some kind of strategic fit, or relevance, to their existing business. This could be as a result of 'vertical integration' opportunities (see Chapter 1) or may relate to location, customer base or market share. It may help to use a brief case study to demonstrate the importance of 'strategic' issues when assessing the value a business may have.

The car dealership

Consider the case of a German-car dealership in the North of England. It had very low net assets, held an expensive long-term lease on its showroom, had traded for some time at a modest loss, and was sapping the energies of its owner who has basically had enough of the car industry. What would you advise him to do? Most of the valuation models that you will uncover within this chapter would suggest the business has no value. After all, it is not generating profit and has few assets. Perhaps it would be best for the owner to dispose of all the assets, hope this raises enough cash to pay off creditors, and try to do a deal with the landlord in handing back the lease early. Is this what you would advise?

What actually happened is that the business was sold as a going concern and realized somewhere in the region of £750,000 for its owner. Why did someone pay such a sum for an unprofitable business? The answer is that the acquiring business had a need to open a new dealership in the North of England as part of its strategic growth plan. It obviously examined the dealership in question and decided it would be cheaper and easier to acquire and develop the existing business rather than launch a new venture in the area from a standing start. Clearly the new owners believe that they can sell more, charge more and spend less than the present owners (or deliver improvements through some mixture of these activities). The key learning from this brief story is that when it comes to valuations, 'it's about them, not you', which is a theme that will arise several times throughout this book.

Don't assume that your loss-making low-asset business is worthless – at least until all possibilities have been examined.

EXTERNALS

There are many external factors that could affect the success and potential value of your business, and by definition these will be largely outside of your control. Some industry sectors are heavily regulated by government, and statutory changes may impact to a significant extent. One example would be the waste management industry, where new legislation often presents threats and opportunities. Obviously it is difficult to pre-empt external changes of this kind.

Other external threats arise from competitors, and the emergence of potential competitors. The development of increasing levels of competition may significantly affect your judgement on the best time to exit your business. Of course, external factors can be positive too. For example, during the 1980s estate agencies were being bought up by mortgage lenders keen to vertically integrate their business. The basic idea was they would sell the house, sell the mortgage and then sell insurance and other related products. In the excitement of vertically integrating, inflated prices were paid for established estate agency businesses.

BARRIERS TO ENTRY

Barriers to entry into your particular sector may play a very significant part in your exit strategy, and also affect how valuable your business appears to others. Some sectors have quite extensive entry barriers. For example, it would be very difficult to set up a new high street bank, given the need for huge amounts of capital, extensive premises, large numbers of staff, and a long-standing reputation. However, it would be easier to set up an internet-based business that offered loans. By definition many sectors that include a large proportion of small businesses (therefore obviously not including retail banking) have relatively low barriers to entry.

Consider an example. To set up as a web designer you just need to go on a training course to provide the necessary technical skills, buy a laptop and some software, and you're in business. Not too many hurdles to leap over. If you consider the car dealership case study above, it will be clear that the barriers to entering the German-car sales market in the North of

England were such that a South-based competitor was happy to pay a significant sum just to enter the market via an established operation.

VALUATION METHODS

There may be countless methods of valuing a business, depending on the circumstances pertaining in each specific case. In the car dealership situation perhaps the approach used was the 'What's it worth to us?' method (not a method at all, just an answer to a question), or maybe the 'entry cost' approach (covered below) was considered. Perhaps the best advice is that you consider each method in turn and evaluate what each predicts about the potential value of your business. It would be wise to do this in conjunction with your accountant. Why? Well, this leads to the most popular method of valuing smaller businesses, the 'multiple' method. When examining this approach, hopefully you will appreciate that while the method is simple, it is possible to manipulate the figures to achieve very diverse outcomes. An experienced accountant should be able to advise on the most appropriate approach for your particular business. (If you are wondering how 'experienced accountant' might be defined, see Chapter 4 on 'Professional Advisers'.)

The multiple values method

The multiple values method of valuing a business is both easy to understand and offers a way for both buyer and seller to evaluate the worth of a business in simple terms. All of the professional advisers I spoke to in preparing this book referred directly to this method. Basically, the post-tax profit of your business (usually referred to in accountancy-speak as 'profit on ordinary activities after taxation' – you will find this at the bottom of your profit and loss account) is multiplied by 'x' times to arrive at the sale figure. Let us take a brief example:

Post-tax profit:　£75,000
Agreed multiple:　× 6
Sale price:　£75,000 × 6 = £450,000

Easy to understand, isn't it? But you may be asking where I got the figure for the multiple from. Of course I made it up, but in reality that is what people do. In conducting my research I asked lawyers, accountants and bank managers what they considered a sensible range of multiples to be. In general there was quite a broad consensus. 'About four to eight times profits', advised an accountant. 'Around five to ten times profits', said a lawyer. 'Usually about four to eight times profits', suggested a bank manager.

There are two important caveats to give to this seemingly consistent advice. First, it depends on the sector in which your business operates. If you run an IT/telecoms business your multiple may be up to 25 times current post-tax profits (or more). Other sectors may have their own unique 'multiple level'. An experienced accountant will have access to information on multiples across a range of sectors, and hopefully will be able to add his or her own experience to this to help identify the appropriate figure pertaining to your specific case. The second point is equally important. A modest increase (or decrease) in the multiplier changes the sale figure very dramatically. To continue with our example above:

Multiple of 4 x profits

Post-tax profit: £75,000
Agreed multiple: × 4
Sale price: £75,000 × 4 = £300,000

Multiple of 8 x profits

Post-tax profit: £75,000
Agreed multiple: × 8
Sale price: £75,000 × 8 = £600,000

Achieving the 'correct' multiple is crucial in maximizing the sale price. Too high, and you might not sell. Too low and you are handing value to the buyer.

The other factor to consider is how you calculate post-tax profits. Surely this figure at least is fixed? Absolutely not. An accountant can help you consider a number of legal ways to influence the final figure. Let's take a simple example. Perhaps you are running a parcels business that is making £75,000 profit (the figure used in the examples above). Let us say you are paying yourself a salary of £40,000 and have been taking bonuses of £30,000 per annum. If you were to drop your salary to £30,000 and take no bonus the recorded net profit figure of the business would rise to (approximately) £115,000. Let's do the eight-times multiple again.

Multiple of 8 x profits

Post tax profit: £115,000
Agreed multiple: × 8
Sale price: £115,000 × 8 = £920,000

This example might be very simplistic, but it shows the importance of examining all of the costs in your business.

Most prospective purchasers will not want a multiple based solely on last year's profit (unless this benefits them). They will probably want the average of the last three years to be taken into account. This is just one of the reasons that you should begin discussions with your accountant as early as possible ahead of the sale. He or she may be able to advise on a number of ways to (legally and properly) restate higher profits. After all, the role of an accountant is to help you to minimize taxable profits legally. I list below just a few of the common ways in which profits may be adjusted. Some may be of relevance in your circumstances:

▌ Your business currently picks up personal non-business expenses such as an expensive car, travel costs or phone costs. If you paid for some of these costs personally, how much would be added to profit (and what would be the result once a 'multiple' has been applied)?
▌ Your business may have recently faced non-recurring costs that have effectively depressed stated profits.
▌ If business premises are owned by you personally, rent may currently be being paid by the business.
▌ The assets of the business may be under- or over-stated and it could be to your advantage to conduct a formal revaluation.

The price/earnings ratio method

The price/earnings ratio ('p/e ratio') method is (in outcome at least) effectively identical to the multiple method, and you may find your professional advisers talk about 'the p/e ratio' rather than 'the multiple method'. However, although the results of the two might be the same, the approach is different. The p/e method is by far the most common approach to evaluating the share price of publicly quoted companies, so it may be worth taking a little time to explain.

Technically the p/e ratio is the *capitalized value* of a business divided by it profits after tax. (If you are interested in a very technical definition, the p/e ratio can be expressed as 'the share price divided by post-tax earnings per share'. This definition doesn't help us in our current quest, so I will ignore it and move on.) Hopefully you can see why the p/e method is not technically the best way to determine the value of your business because it relies on your already knowing the value of your business! However, if you were to examine a publicly quoted company you would be able to identify its capitalized value by multiplying the number of shares in existence by the share price. Here is a simple example:

Number of shares issued: 1 million
Current price per share: £1.00
Capitalized value of business: £1 million

If the company makes £100,000 per annum post-tax profits the p/e ratio gives the following results:

Price (capitalized value):   £1 million
Earnings (post-tax profit):   £100,000
p/e ratio: £1 million/£100,000 = 10 times

This is basically analogous to having a multiple of 10. After all, if your business makes £100,000 post-tax profit and you agree to sell for a multiple of 10, you will be valuing your business at £1 million. Why is it useful to understand the p/e method? Because you can benchmark your business against larger competitors within your sector.

Say you own a medium-sized catering firm. You could find a number of larger catering businesses that have their shares listed on the stock exchange (or on the Alternative Investments Market, which is basically a stock market for smaller or less-established businesses) and work out their p/e ratio from information that is easily available on the internet, or by accessing their own published accounts and annual reports. This should be useful in helping to think about the p/e ratio of your business. After all, they are providing information about how the market values a catering business. You do need to be careful, however, because publicly quoted companies usually have a much higher p/e ratio than smaller unquoted counterparts. Perhaps the key reason behind this is that it is much easier to buy and sell shares in a quoted company, which in turn makes their shares much more attractive to investors. It has been suggested to me that the effective p/e ratio for a small private company could be 50 per cent lower than that of a comparable publicly quoted company that operates in the same business sector, but of course this will not apply universally.

Another interesting fact is that the stock market appears to value 'smaller' firms higher that 'larger' ones. For example, the FTSE 100, which represents the 100 largest UK publicly quoted companies, has an average p/e ratio of around 13. The FTSE 250 index, however, which is made up of the largest 250 shares, has an average ratio of around 19. Why should there be a 50 per cent difference? If I knew the answer, I would be a professional investor rather than writer-cum-jobbing consultant; however, here is a guess. Perhaps the biggest 100 firms are unlikely to be takeover targets because of their sheer size. To buy 100 per cent of Tesco shares you would need at least £34 billion, and there aren't too many predators which have that much ready cash (at least who would want to buy a supermarket). However, smaller plcs (which are still very big businesses) might be much more vulnerable to takeovers from private equity firms, and this might be factored in by the markets.

Another consideration is to examine a number of shares within the same sector to get a feel for the spread of p/e. For example, Tesco plc (on the day I checked) had a p/e ratio of 19.3, whereas William Morrison plc had a p/e of 13.4. Clearly the people who buy retail shares currently value Tesco much more highly than Morrison's. This type of analysis can be helpful, as it gives you information and ideas. However, the fact that share prices diverge so markedly (and change so quickly) should convince you that speaking to an experienced accountant (who can help you understand the fundamental value within your business) is important. Getting the ratio right is crucial to achieving a profitable sale.

Asset valuation method

If you add up all of the assets of your business, and then subtract all liabilities, you will be left with a figure. In fact, your accountant does this each year-end in producing the balance sheet for inclusion in your annual accounts. However, unless your business is heavily capital-intensive (perhaps a property business or manufacturing company), it is unlikely that this will be the most effective valuation method. As we discussed earlier, businesses in the modern economy rely increasingly on 'knowledge' and 'information' rather than large capital assets, and this has changed over time. A hundred years ago most large and successful businesses required expensive assets. Think of railways, steelworks or international transport companies. But many of today's global businesses rely on information, market knowledge or intangible marketing 'capital'. Consider Microsoft or even Coca-Cola. Much of their value is to some extent intangible (at least by traditional methods) but is no less 'real' for being so.

Many small businesses have few tangible assets beyond office equipment, yet have significant value. Many of the most successful businesses in the United Kingdom over the last decade have developed in service or knowledge-based sectors. An example would be the rise of the recruitment business. Some have few assets yet have sold for very large sums. The key point here is that even though you may run a manufacturing business that holds significant assets, it may not be sensible to rely on the asset base to generate the valuation figure. I know of one medium-sized manufacturing business where the owner has a five-year plan to sell. The asset value of the business is significant, but the directors realize that a much higher valuation would be achieved not by expanding assets, but by increasing the profit capability of the business through developing value-added services. For this reason most of their planned investment relates to developing IT solutions that will add value for customers and allow them to grow turnover through subcontracting services effectively.

Perhaps the most common situation where the asset valuation method is used relates to a 'forced sale', or situations where a company is not profitable but must be sold quickly. If you have to exit a loss-making business, realizing the asset value may be the best route available to you. However, there is no guarantee that you will achieve the asset figure stated in the accounts (known as the 'net book value'). Auction values for equipment (and sometimes even property) are often well below the net book value figure.

Entry cost valuation method

One way that a potential purchaser may determine the value of your business is to compare your asking price with the cost of setting up a similar business from scratch. Perhaps the purchaser of the German-car dealership did so. Unsurprisingly, to do this accurately is quite a task. Obviously certain factors will be reasonably predictable. For example, the cost of office space, equipment – even recruiting and employing staff – may not be too difficult to judge. However, the cost associated with developing products or in growing market share and creating a loyal customer base may be extremely challenging to estimate – for both for the potential buyer and yourself.

This situation requires a comparative analysis of the cost of purchase versus the cost of developing a business from the ground up. The following simple analysis may be useful in determining whether your business may be attractively valued using this method. If you complete the exercise and find the result attractive it may be worth investigating the entry costs to your sector in more detail, which may assist in developing a longer-term exit strategy.

Activity: Simple entry cost valuation

First calculate the value of your business using the multiple method. If your business is asset-rich you may also find it useful to estimate a realistic value based on total assets less current liabilities (the figure will be shown in your accounts). This will give you the basis for comparing how variable the figures are when utilizing different approaches.

Now list all of the elements that would be required to replicate your business. Begin with the easy factors and gradually consider less tangible aspects. Your 'easy' list may include:

▌ cost of leasing premises (if you own the freehold calculate the likely cost of someone leasing the premises from you);
▌ cost of machinery;
▌ cost of office equipment and stationery;
▌ cost of furnishings and fittings.

The 'more difficult to quantify' list may include:

▌ marketing costs;
▌ sales activity required to build up a comparable customer base;
▌ cost of employing yourself and others until revenue comes into the business to cover your costs (also called 'working capital');
▌ lost sales during this period (if they bought your business rather than developing one from scratch they would presumably enjoy sales at around the current level from day one).

Now add up all of these costs. How does the figure compare with the 'multiple' or asset valuation calculations? Does this tell you anything about the potential value of your business?

Net present value method

In the Introduction I wrote that an accountant might suggest that 'Your business is worth its net present value (as determined by the balance sheet) plus the net present value of all future known revenues.' What does this mean in English? I guess that the best way to describe this approach is to say that it is very much like the asset valuation method but includes future predictable additions to the balance sheet.

For example, if you have a business that has a reliable revenue stream (with long-term contracts in place) and where costs are under control, it will be possible to predict not just future revenue flows but also future profitability. (This is obviously an ideal situation, whatever valuation method is used.) A simplified scenario is set out below:

If your business currently has net assets of £100,000 and it can be predicted that profits of £10,000 per annum will be achieved over the next five years, you might conclude that a purchaser would be prepared to value the business at £150,000 (which covers the current asset valuation, plus the predicted profits for five years). This approach could be seen as a kind of amalgam of the asset valuation model and the multiple model, but the figure generated is higher than either method on their own would deliver. However, it might occur to you that £10,000 next year is not worth quite as much as £10,000 today. Adjustment would have to be made for inflation, which could be a significant factor over a period of five years. In fact, even assuming a modest inflation rate of about 3 per cent, the £10,000 in year five would only be worth about £8,500 at today's prices. Your accountant will use a mathematical formula to demonstrate the value of future money at today's prices and the technical term for doing so is the 'net present value'. Similarly, you will also need to take into account depreciation or indeed increases in asset values.

This approach is also referred to as the 'discounted cash flow method'. One slight variation on the approach may involve a calculation of all future dividends payable over the time period in question, plus an estimate of the residual asset value at the end of the period. Put simply, the approach estimates how much money you would receive in dividend payments over X years, plus how much the business will be worth at that time. This does of course present the headache that you have to be able to calculate the value of the business at a later date. As we have seen, it is not necessarily easy to do so in the present – predicting future value may be even more challenging!

SECTOR RULES OF THUMB

In some sectors, factors other than profit may be used to calculate approximate sale values. Occasionally a situation develops where the sector can be said to have a 'rules of thumb' approach. For example, if you have a computer maintenance business there may be a rule of thumb that suggests the sale value would be either X times revenue or even X times the number of maintenance contracts held. In other sectors, the number of customers may be crucial. For example, if you have an internet insurance business that has 20,000 customers a prospective purchaser might know how much it costs for their current business to acquire an additional customer (through marketing-related expenditure). If this figure is £400, your business would be worth 20,000 × £400 = £800,000 (if you happen to be in the insurance business don't rely on this figure being at all accurate – I made it up by way of example).

An experienced accountant should be in a position to help examine any potential rules of thumb possibilities. Generally this approach works best where you operate a business to consumer company (B2C), rather than business to business (B2B). B2C companies tend to have large numbers of customers who each spend a relatively small amount. B2B companies often have relatively few customers who represent a larger proportion of revenue. Of course, this is just a rule of thumb!

HOW THE BIG BOYS DO IT

Your business could be worth a few thousand pounds or perhaps a few million. But some businesses are valued at literally billions of pounds. Clearly the advice contained within this book is not aimed at very large organizations, which have armies of bankers, lawyers, accountants and other specialists on call to help them at any time. However, it may be enlightening for the rest of us to understand how the largest organizations approach the process of calculating their own value, and how they prepare ahead of a business sale.

When large organizations offer shares for sale into the wider market the process is known as an Initial Purchase Offering (IPO). You will probably be more familiar with the term 'flotation', which is the word often used when a privately owned business offers shares to financial institutions and the wider public through becoming listed on a stock exchange. The London Stock Exchange is one of the most important bodies of its kind in the world and many of the most familiar large business have their shares listed on it. During the 1980s and 1990s the UK government 'floated' a number of previously public owned organizations on the London Stock Exchange through the process of an IPO. British Telecom and British Gas are perhaps the best remembered examples. Obviously most IPOs do not have such a high profile as these examples, which famously involved businesses owned by the government (on behalf of the public) being sold into private ownership. In fact, many IPOs are never heard of outside of the corporate finance sector, and are only mentioned in the *Financial Times* and other specialist financial media.

There are many reasons why the owners of a large private business would wish to sell at least some of their shares as part of an IPO. Perhaps the present owners wish to 'cash in' and realize some real monetary value for their shareholdings. Alternatively, big businesses see IPOs as an attractive method of raising finance for expansion compared to borrowing money from banks or doing a deal with a private equity firm or venture capitalist (who may want a say in how the business operates in future, and therefore place onerous obligations on the directors).

When the directors of a very large company decide to raise capital by selling some (or all) of the organization's shares via an IPO they face the same questions – and challenges – that you encounter in your more modest business. How much is the business worth? Who would be interested in buying shares? How should they market their offering? Which professional advisers would provide the best support? When would be the best time to act? The fact that the values of their organizations contain several more noughts than your business does not appear to affect the nature of the questions that need to be answered. However, whilst the questions are the same, the process of finding answers will be somewhat different to the approach that you take.

The first point of difference is that the primary professional adviser a large organization relies on to support it throughout the process tends to be an investment bank. Investment banks operate in a world of large financial deals. They have regular contacts with organizations that manage pensions and investment funds, ie have interests in large businesses, and also wealthy individuals – in short the people who count when large amounts of money are invested. If your business is worth hundreds of millions (or billions), speaking to an investment bank may be the best place to start, as it has access to 'buyers' with extremely deep pockets.

Earlier in this chapter we discussed a variety of approaches to valuing a business but included a caveat that overall the real value is what someone is prepared to pay. The same approach applies to very large organizations – only the total figure, and therefore cash variations between estimates, become much larger. The process that investment banks use for valuing businesses vary, and some approaches are masked in secrecy, but in general they have two weapons at their disposal that their customers don't. First, they can benchmark the business against similar organizations that have issued shares through an IPO. Although much of this information would be publicly available (it is a 'public offering' after all), the ability to financially compare two very different organizations from a valuation perspective is a challenging task requiring both knowledge and experience. The second approach they may utilize is to speak to a broad range of people within the financial community, to gain a wider perspective. If a large number of fund managers believe the business is valuable and would be worth investing in, the IPO is likely to be a success. After all, they are the people who control the cash that would buy the shares.

The IPO road show

In researching this book I spoke to someone with over 20 years' experience working in large financial institutions, who now earns a living by helping to influence the initial share price of large businesses through an IPO road show. The process he describes for marketing the shares is something like this. Imagine you are CEO of a very large business that wants to raise £1 billion through the public offering of half of the company's shares. You have liaised with investment banks, and appointed teams of solicitors, accountants and other advisers. You have been advised that the initial share price of your business would be in the range of £9.00 to £11.00 per share, which would generate (for example) between £900 million and £1,100 million. The difference between the higher price and lower price is £200 million! Obviously it is worth investing time, money and effort to ensure that the final valuation is much nearer the top end of the range than the bottom. So you appoint a team of people who arrange for you to jet around all of the European capitals (plus the odd trip to New York and Tokyo), speaking to investment fund managers, pension fund managers and all manner of other people who control large amounts of cash, to sell the idea that buying shares in your business represents an excellent investment opportunity.

This process may sound pretty glamorous to those of us who operate on a much more mundane level. Surely it must be fantastic to travel in private jets and stay in five-star hotel rooms, with every aspect of your day taken care of by the team of people whose job it is to ensure everything goes smoothly. Well, that is one way of looking at it. The other way is to consider giving 70 identical presentations in a dozen countries in less that a fortnight, whilst being consistently interrogated by people who hold it within their power to make your share offering a huge success or dismal failure. This latter point is important. You have spent a year of your time and staked your professional reputation on raising £1 billion, yet find yourself exhausted, in the cramped compartment of a private plane being served lukewarm food whilst you prepare for your 38th meeting of the week, and your body is screaming that it needs to sleep. (I almost feel sorry for these people, but then I remind myself what they earn.)

The investment story

Obviously the jetting around is important, but of much greater relevance is the 'story' that is being communicated. When talking to people involved in the world of 'high finance' it is easy to become overawed by the jargon they use, and I won't embarrass myself by trying to explain it here. Fundamentally the 'investment story' aims to explain how and why the business makes money, and how and why it will continue to make money in the future. Communicating this may involve multi-coloured graphs, complex financial models and futuristic projections, but the underlying message is very straightforward. And the reasons that their business makes money and will continue to do so are identical to those that pertain to your much more modest business: finding and keeping customers, differentiating products, controlling costs, employing skilled and motivated staff, ensuring income is contracted, appointing the best managers, investing wisely in technology, understanding the changes that are happening in the marketplace, innovating in how business is transacted and so on. For them the prize for getting this message right is a successful sale at the top end of the valuation range – and this is exactly comparable with your objective when selling your business.

CREATING YOUR OWN INVESTMENT STORY

Creating the 'investment story' (or explaining why people would want to buy your business) is a crucial early step in achieving a successful sale. Its primary purpose could be to explain as clearly as possible how your business generates profits, and why it will continue to do so. Some of the factors behind this may relate to a 'unique model' that you have within your business, and other factors may be externalized – perhaps you have a long-term sole-rights agreement to distribute a certain product range in the UK. In considering your investment story it is important to look outwards as well as inwards. Several times in this book we have alluded to the fact that selling a business is about 'them': your potential purchasers. What factors will influence them? It could be that your business makes very modest profits but has a significant number of customers. Perhaps access to customers is what will most excite a potential buyer and would therefore be a key part of your investment story.

I have a friend who successfully earns his living through helping businesses communicate better both internally and externally. He believes that all businesses are extremely simple at the most basic level. His advice is always to focus on creating happy customers who will give you money. Too obvious? His experience is that many businesses lose sight of this and get wrapped up in busy day-to-day routines that contribute little to generating happy customers, which is the only activity underpinning commercial success. His view is that the investment story should focus most energy on explaining how happy customers are created and maintained, and how this could be further developed by the new owner. I guess we have all seen advertisements for 'businesses for sale' that suggest 'significant scope for expansion/development/sales increase'. In successfully selling your business it is not enough to merely suggest this. You need to be in a position to explain how it can be achieved. This is the investment story.

The remainder of this section aims to help you consider the key elements of your investment story. The approach has two aspects. First, to think about all of the aspects of the business that could play an important part in the story, and secondly to reduce these into cogent and compelling arguments that are simple to articulate and quantify.

Activity: Creating your investment story

Chapter 5 will explore how to construct a document known as the 'sale memorandum'. This is a document that sets out key information about your business and the marketplace in which it operates. The document is specifically intended to be of interest to potential buyers or investors. Before you get to the stage of preparing the memorandum it might be useful to begin thinking about the story behind your business. Could you explain to someone in just a couple of minutes why your business generates happy customers? Why are they happy to hand over their hard-earned money to you? Why will this process continue in the future? Why will you achieve this despite the efforts of competitors? What is unique about your approach? (Perhaps nothing is unique: you are merely very efficient at what you do.)

Take time now to write down the answers to these questions. Don't worry about the format at this stage – no one will see it and you will be guided through a structured approach to creating a formal document later.

Having drafted answers to these questions, consider adding figures. Look historically at how your business has (hopefully) grown and developed. Link the figures into the story in a way that gives credibility and support to the key messages. For example, has turnover grown over the last three years? Have you managed to reduce costs in the business? Is profitability up? In as few words as possible explain how and why these improvements happened. Don't worry about creating a long document; a couple of paragraphs will do. You are aiming to produce something that could be said in about two minutes that would generate interest in the listener. To help you get the feel of the output, here is a fictitious 'two-minute' investment story.

The event business

In just six years 'Shocking Events' has become the leading creative force in the provision of live corporate communications in the North East. From humble beginnings in a 'back bedroom', the business has grown turnover year on year, culminating in £7 million revenues during the last 12 months, and our biggest-ever event attracted, managed, fed and entertained crowds of 17,000 people.

Most of our new business comes from word-of-mouth recommend-ations. We have over 40 'live clients' (including three FTSE 100 organizations) and added 10 new ones during the last year. We are proud that our first ever customer remains an enthusiastic user of our services. Profitability has grown in real terms year on year to a point where pre-tax profitability topped £1 million last year. Profits are reinvested or used to reward our loyal and dedicated team.

Our uniqueness is achieved through attracting and retaining the best creative brains, coupled with robust business processes that ensure we deliver on time and on budget – always.

Our value proposition is based on 'being the best' at a price comparable to the rest of the market (and significantly lower than most London-centric competitors). We will never be the cheapest, but clients understand they get excellent creative input coupled with solid project management skills.

Our mission? Happy corporate customers who choose us again and again.

In about 200 words I hope I have managed to convey quite a lot about the fictitious business in question. Of course, this isn't a fully developed investment story, but if I worked it up – adding key financial figures and providing well-considered projections – I am confident that an interesting proposition could be developed. Notice how the past, present and future are mentioned. Prospective buyers will be interested in how the business has developed, and how it will continue to progress. Also consider that much of the content is factual and includes headline numbers. It focuses on why the business succeeds and quantifies success – for example by referring to the number of new clients acquired in the past 12 months. It mentions the quality of staff and philosophically states its mission. It also touches on project management skills and creativity. Quite a lot of positive information for around 200 words.

If you allow yourself a maximum of two pages of A4 paper, you should be able to construct a compelling investment story that includes historical figures and well-considered projections. And you will have done so in about 1,000 words.

Chapter 5 contains many more ideas of how to attract interest in your business, and will provide a structure for the 'sale memorandum', which is basically the investment story in a structured format.

Chapter summary

▊ Valuing a business is an art, not a science. A business is worth what someone will pay for it.

▊ Potential customers will be encouraged to offer a higher valuation if they can understand how the business will (or will continue to) *sell more, charge more or spend less.* These are the ingredients that add up to profitability.

▊ Other important factors include having a model for generating sustainable profits, considering whether your business fits the buyer in some strategic sense, and how difficult (costly) it would be to replicate your business from scratch.

▊ There are a variety of valuation methods and you should examine all of them. Each may tell you something about the potential value of your business.

▊ In the modern economy, competitive advantage is often found in data, design and creativity, and in harnessing innovative ways of exploiting information, rather than building bigger factories or storing up ever greater amounts of capital. Whatever your business, creatively manipulating information may add significant value.

▊ The largest businesses face the same valuation issues that you do. They invest a great deal of time creating their investment story. You should do the same. (See Chapter 6 for more ideas.)

3

Developing an Exit Strategy

The economist John Maynard Keynes once remarked that 'in the long run we are all dead'. I use this happy thought to bring home the fact that one day you will not run your business. You may stay involved with the business until they have to carry you out, but one day you will leave. In fact, having read this book thus far you are obviously contemplating leaving, or at least planning for a time when you wish to depart. This chapter deals with the planning aspect.

There are many reasons for people exiting a business, including:

▌ a planned retirement;
▌ a desire to hand control to children or others;
▌ cashing in (many business owners have most of their wealth tied up in the company);
▌ threats to the business (new competitors or legislation may convince you that now is the time to go);
▌ ill health;
▌ boredom (the desire to do something else with your life);
▌ divorce (perhaps your partner has decided to do something else with his or her life).

You will have your own reasons for leaving at what you consider the right moment, and of course factors do change over time. Perhaps you always hoped that your daughter would become involved in your car-hire business but she has rebelled and gone to law school. Not all things are within your control, and certainly not teenage sons and daughters. The key point is to think flexibly and prepare for change through time.

Nevertheless, you must prepare an exit strategy and allow it to evolve.

In planning ahead, the single most important factor is to be clear as to your objectives. Be absolutely clear what you would like to happen and when. Any objectives should include having clarity regarding:

I   your aspiration for the sale price of your business;
I   the timescale for exiting your business;
I   the target market of potential buyers;
I   practical ideas for maximizing the value of your business;
I   how you will manage the exit process.

SET THE PARAMETERS OF SUCCESS

Your first objective should relate to your aspiration for the sale price. How much money do you need? You may decide that a jet-set lifestyle complete with yacht, private plane and houses on three continents is essential. However, if you currently run a small tool-hire business in Dewsbury, you probably have some expanding to do ahead of the sale. Conversely, if your spending requirements are modest and you just want to create time to write a novel or learn to play the didgeridoo, your life may be enhanced by leaving your business sooner rather than later. No one (and certainly not I) will be able to determine these issues for you because we are talking about *your* life. But if you can make your business successful, and have a structured plan to sell at some point, your life options will be significantly enhanced.

In Chapter 2 we examined various methods for valuing a business, and suggested that you sense-check any resulting figures with a know-ledgeable person who can remain objective. You accountant would be a good starting point, although bank managers can provide a solid sounding board, and they often cost less (on an informal basis) than an accountant. If your financial aspirations significantly exceed the expected sale value, radical decisions may be needed. Should you expand the current business? Should you sell the current business for whatever you can achieve now and invest your money and resources in another business or sector? Should you cut costs to boost short-term profitability (and will this deliver a higher sale price)?

Whatever the situation, the key requirement is 'ruthless objectivity' on your part. If you want millions in the bank but currently run a fledgling business, you probably have a great deal of hard work ahead of you. Dreams are wonderful and help keep us motivated, but your bank won't allow them to be deposited in a working account. This book suggests a number of shortcuts that can help boost the value of your business, but you must live in the real world. If your business has a medium-term plan for growth and profitability, your exit strategy should tie in closely with it.

Activity: Make a list

What do *you* want to achieve in financial terms and when? Write it down now. How much money do you want to make? How quickly do you need to make it? In doing so it will be helpful to remain in the real world rather than Utopia. You might, for example, have written that you want £10 million tomorrow. Unfortunately, the next question I will ask is 'What was the value that you put on your business as a result of the exercises in Chapter 2?' Obviously, if your figure was £50,000 you are going to have to find £9,950,000 within the next 24 hours, which may be a little challenging. Of course this is not to say you can't one day have a business worth £10 million, but tomorrow probably isn't that day. Reflect realistically on the effort that will be required and over what time period. Write something down. We will review your figure and underlying assumptions towards the end of the book.

THE TIME TO MAKE A PROFIT IS…

When I run workshops in commercial negotiation techniques I often witness people acting in very strange ways. One common occurrence is that following a poor negotiation with a disastrous result, people explain away the difficulties by saying 'Of course next time I meet this supplier/ customer/whatever, I will get a much better result.' My stock response in such situations is to say, 'Excellent, I'm glad you learnt from this but the *time to make a profit is now*, not next time.'

Making a profit *now* has become a bit of a mantra for me, but is it good advice when it comes to selling your business? Not necessarily. There are many successful business people who keep investing in and growing their business to meet some long-term plan – in some cases aspiring to float on the stock market via an initial public offering. Why don't they just get out now with enough money to last a lifetime? I'm afraid it is down to personal choice and levels of aspiration. However, we need to take into account the importance of timing in maximizing the result. In the introduction to this book I briefly mentioned a business that went from being valued at over £2 million to £1 in less than a year. How hard has the owner of that business been kicking himself ever since? Why didn't he attempt to sell at the high point? Obviously he believed the business could be worth even more in the future, but that is one clear instance where my suggestion that 'the time to make a profit is now' would have been very apt. In order to balance this story it is worth considering the situation where someone exited a business too early.

On the rack

Bryan ran a medium-sized racking business that provided storage solutions for warehouses. He developed the business over an eight-year period. Whilst the business achieved modest year on year growth, it struggled to successfully develop large national accounts. When the opportunity came along to sell the business to a company involved in supermarket shelving, he more or less snatched its hand off and quickly agreed the sale at quite a modest price.

The new owners had contacts in the supermarket sector and were able to promote the racking business into a number of major national retailers. Turnover and profitability grew by a factor of five times over three years. The new owners sold the business to a large national organization and made a huge profit.

What did Bryan do wrong? Perhaps nothing. But it could be argued that he had put in most of the hard work in getting the business off the ground and in his eagerness to sell to the first person to express an interest had given up the opportunity to achieve perhaps four or five times the value. The new owners did bring something new to the table (their contacts), but it would not have been impossible for Bryan to break into the market. Of course, he may have been happy to get out when he did, and his golf handicap has probably improved in the intervening period.

TARGETING POTENTIAL BUYERS

In Chapter 1 we considered a broad range of people – or organizations – that may be interested in buying your business. The list of possibilities includes employees, customers and competitors in addition to people as yet unknown. Even if you are several years away from your anticipated disposal date, it is sensible to investigate and plan your approach to attracting potential buyers. Of course, this does not just involve writing things down on paper. For example, if one potential outcome is a management buyout (MBO) it may make sense to start grooming members of your management team ahead of time. Perhaps you could delegate tasks to certain key people, or involve them more in strategic decisions. This may help warm them up to the idea that they could profitably take over and run the business. All of this can be done in a covert way. You don't have to drag your sales manager in on Monday morning and tell her 'Julie, I'm thinking of getting out in a couple of years and want to involve you more in the business so you can lead the team who buys it from me.' Of course, you may want to speak in this way at some point, as one of the team will need to take the lead in an MBO situation.

A gentler approach may involve 'Julie' and other colleagues becoming more involved in key meetings and decisions and being trusted with commercially sensitive information. The idea of sharing sensitive information with employees may fill you with horror. Obviously some information is too sensitive to share some of the time, but most of us will have worked in an environment where information is cascaded using the mushroom principle ('keep them in the dark and feed them bullshit') and realize the problems this can create. In my role as a management consultant I often have initial sales meetings with finance directors of potential clients. In these meetings I typically ask lots of questions about the products purchased by the company and how it spends money. On many occasions finance directors (of large firms, sometimes plcs) print out and hand over their management accounts to me. It always amazes me that an intelligent and qualified senior manager is prepared to share hard data with me on a first meeting that would not be shared with almost all employees of the client's own firm. Obviously I like to think I have an honest face and have never betrayed a trust. Nevertheless, it seems that trusting plausible strangers is often easier that trusting long-term employees. My experience is that trust is paid back in equal measure, which may be something to consider whilst planning ahead to a potential MBO.

Perhaps an MBO isn't an option for you, with more likely prospective purchasers being competitors or customers. There are still things that can be done to ensure that they develop a warm interest in your business, without creating problems for you. One of the most effective ways is a structured public relations (PR) programme that lets interested parties know that you exist and are doing well. Some people consider PR to be an exercise in spinning half truths, peddled by slimy politicians and their advisers. PR does not have to be like that. First, as will be detailed in Chapter 5, you can handle PR effectively yourself (without the slime and on a small budget). Secondly, the world (or at least your customers, competitors and suppliers) will be interested to find out how your business is doing. The key point is to consider *now* whom the future buyer of your business might be and plan for making yourself known to them. Ensure you target potential buyers as soon as possible. Doing so will maximize the time you have to influence them, whether by subtle or direct methods.

Should you consider your business too small or insignificant to warrant a structured strategy for targeting potential buyers, think again. The most modest business can benefit from a methodical approach, as the story of Ray will confirm.

The print shop

Ray ran a small high-street print shop that produced business cards, letterheads and general commercial stationery. He also had another business venture, which was proving more lucrative and was taking up a disproportionate amount of time. He decided to sell the print shop.

Having spoken to a number of business brokers he decided on a two-pronged strategy. First, he would formally advertise the business through a broker, being prepared to sell either the business assets separately from the freehold property, or sell the business and property as a whole. The second part of his strategy was to use his extensive network of contacts, informing all of them of his plans at every opportunity. He bored friends, relations and business contacts to good effect. The business was sold not through a business broker but through his physiotherapist. Whilst lying on his back being pummelled, Ray explained about the business being for sale and asked if the physiotherapist had any other clients who might be interested. He did, and they bought the shop.

If we put this strange but true story into a strategic context, Ray did a lot of things right. First, he did not just rely on a business broker; he used his existing contacts and experience to supplement the formal approach to selling. Secondly, he was prepared to share some information with a broad range of people – after all, how can anyone help if they don't have basic facts? Thirdly, he realized that business people form a very broad church. He didn't just see his physiotherapist as the man who attacks him for money every Tuesday, but as a business person with local commercial contacts. Build informal contacts into your plan for targeting potential buyers.

PLANNING AHEAD TO MAXIMIZE VALUE

If you began this book at the beginning and are reading through in sequence you will have encountered a variety of ideas to help you maximize the sale price of your business. If you are jumping from chapter to chapter as the fancy takes you and have not read through Chapter 2, it would be a good idea to do so now before progressing further. The key message from that chapter (but read the whole chapter anyway) is that although there are many ways of valuing a business, ultimately the final value is based on what others are prepared to pay. As shown in Chapter 2, people can be influenced to pay more for a business when faced with a full long-term order book and a broad customer base.

Having encountered these ideas you should now be considering how and when you can make changes that will significantly add value to the sale price. For example, do you have customers without formal contracts? If so, it may be a good idea to think about formalizing all contracts, and having this completed ahead of any planned sale. Consider the following advertisements for the sale of a window cleaning round.

Window cleaning round for sale
Baddon Green area. Ladder and bucket included.
Tel: 000 000000 0000. Ask for Phil.

Window cleaning round for sale
Includes contracts covering over 150 properties.
Consistent and growing customer base.
Very profitable with further possibility for development.
Tel: 000 000000 0000. Ask for Phil.

OK, so I have used a slightly ridiculous example in a vain attempt to amuse you, but if I were a window cleaner who wanted to sell my round I would ensure I had names and addresses of all customers and have contracts in place for all of them. Of course, when I say 'contract' in this context I don't mean something that includes 50 clauses with titles such as 'Force majeure'. What I have in mind is a single sheet of paper that says Phil the window cleaner will clean the exterior windows once a month for £10, that the money is payable immediately on completion and that one month's notice of termination is required. How much more impressed would you be as a potential buyer of Phil's round if you called around at his house and were presented with a lever arch file with 150 signed agreements? These bits of paper would be a lot more valuable than a free ladder and bucket.

The point is, if you are a window cleaner who plans to retire next year, formalizing your customer base could form a key part of your strategy for maximizing the sale price achieved. Lest you think this advice is limited to window cleaners, it was also a key part of Ray the high-street printer's strategy. When he bought the print business it had a list of about 100 customers (account sales), but the cash customers were unknown. By the time Ray sold the business a few years later the list of known and recorded customers had grown threefold. Plan ahead to add value.

MANAGING YOUR EXIT PROCESS

You should think ahead about how you will leave your business. In your mind you may visualize walking out of the front door carrying a large cheque, which is the simplest and possibly preferred option. However, being realistic, for some types of business it will be difficult to make an immediate and total withdrawal. The following section will help you to think through the various options and implications with a view to allowing you to plan ahead.

There are a number of ways to sell a business, but most will fall into one of four categories:

1. You sell all of your shares and leave the business.
2. You sell all of your shares and continue to work in the business.
3. You sell some of your shares and leave the business.
4. You sell some of your shares and continue to work in the business.

The above may sound obvious, but there are significant implications depending on the situation you find yourself in. Let's take the four scenarios in turn.

1. You sell all of your shares and leave the business

Selling all of your shares to a third party and immediately leaving the business is very straightforward from your point of view, and offers many advantages. You are free to go and pursue your life in whichever way you choose (subject to any competition restrictions, as detailed in Chapter 7). Of course, you have to consider how and when you will be paid for your shares. This crucial point is dealt with a little later in this chapter.

For some types of business this type of arrangement works well for both parties. I once bought a small business and the previous owner stayed on for four weeks whilst we communicated effectively with customers, and then left with a cheque in his pocket. I didn't want him around longer than that, and he certainly didn't want to stay. In some types of business, however, the current owner could be vital to the long-term success of the business, and it may necessary for him or her to stay in the business for quite some time to guarantee continuity and future success.

Think closely about your business. How would a prospective purchaser view your immediate departure? Would it be with joy or anguish? In Chapter 1 I introduced the notion that in selling your business you should focus on *them* (your prospective purchaser) and this is one area where viewing the situation from the other person's perspective is crucial.

2. You sell all of your shares and continue to work in the business

Why continue to work in a business you no longer own? Well, it is not necessarily an attractive proposition but it may be necessary. The usual situation is that you are locked-in for one, two or three years. This is often coupled with part of your pay-out being linked with the ongoing profitability of the business. In other words you remain incentivized because to maximize your payout you have to ensure the business continues to perform. The financial aspect of this is covered in detail a little later; however, it is important to examine the notion of remaining 'incentivized' with reference to you keeping motivated.

Consider the situation. You have built up your business over many years of hard slog. You have dealt with stroppy customers and unreliable employees, cash-flow problems and big investment decisions. In short, you have evolved into a capable, competent, motivated business person and hopefully the financial success of your endeavours has provided significant rewards. All of a sudden you have to transmute back into being 'an employee'. Do not underestimate the culture shock that this process can trigger. Even if you retain your title and sit on your usual chair in the same office, you may feel very differently and the effect on your motivation (and contentment) levels can be very profound. You may have to live with this for three years! Think very carefully about how long you will remain in your business when it becomes someone else's property. Do not underestimate the psychological change that this creates.

3. You sell some of your shares and leave the business

Why would you retain a financial interest in a business you no longer work in? Many reasons are possible, but perhaps the key one is you have faith in the management team and in future profitability. Perhaps you have sold out to an MBO, but the team could not raise enough cash, so you have covered the shortfall by remaining a minority shareholder. In this situation the business is now being run by someone you know and trust.

The best advice in this scenario is 'be pessimistic'. Even if you trust the new management team, ensure you are contractually protected. Otherwise, unless you retain a controlling interest you are no longer in control of major decisions. Being a minority shareholder in a private company usually offers few guaranteed benefits and you should consult a specialist commercial lawyer before moving from a majority to a minority shareholding.

4. You sell some of your shares and continue to work in the business

The caveats in this scenario are covered above. You have lost control and therefore need to think clearly about the implications both financially, and psychologically.

DIFFERENT TYPES OF MONEY

Whatever your situation, the one thing that will be guaranteed to be at the heart of the sale process is *money*. Even if you want to hand over the business to your children free of charge, the Chancellor of the Exchequer will insist monetary considerations are at the forefront of a sale agreement. It is a sad indictment of the complexities of 21st-century life that you can't even give things away without HM Revenue and Customs demanding a cut, but there it is.

In considering different types of money I am not referring to pounds, dollars or euros, even though you may well be paid in any of them (if so, you obviously need to factor in the exchange rate, but that is a straightforward consideration). What I am referring to are things such as 'cash now', 'a promise of cash in the future', 'shares in the acquiring business' and so on. I find it helpful to consider these as different types of money.

Cash now

'Cash is king' as the saying goes, and to become carried away with clichés, 'money in the bank' is, well, money in the bank. It may or may not have something to do with being a Yorkshireman, but my preference is always for money now. You should have a good (and well-considered) reason for preferring other payment options to receiving money at the time of sale. (Of course, when I say 'cash' I don't mean bundles of tenners – a bank transfer will be equally acceptable.) Remember, the time to make a profit is *now*.

Deferred payment

There are many variants on deferred payment, but in principle two options exist. First, deferred payments may be linked to future performance, for example directly linked to future years' profits. If you sell your business and exit immediately you will obviously have very little control over future profits and need to think these issues through carefully. Secondly, deferred payments may be the result of the buyers' inability to pay the full amount now. So if you sell out to an MBO made up of your existing management team, they may not have been able to raise the full sale price and expect to pay the balance in forthcoming years. This scenario usually means the level of cash is linked to profits, and if they don't make enough it will be difficult to pay you. A good lawyer can create a contract that ensures legally they have to pay you, but what happens if they just do not have the money? Taking legal action to recover damages from someone who has no ability to pay usually compounds the problem, rather than resolving it. Be pessimistic and take professional advice.

If the reason behind a deferred payment is genuinely linked to the buyer's inability to access enough funding it may well be worth contacting your local 'business angels' organization. If the name has raised a smile on your face, and you believe I am suggesting heavenly intervention, think again. 'Business angels' is the wonderfully creative name for individuals who have both available resources and business experience, and an interest in investing in smaller businesses. Professional advisers I spoke to in preparing this book suggest that business angels are often very useful where a funding gap exists between the amount of capital a buyer can raise and the sum required to buy the business. Not only can they provide cash, they also have good business experience. Of course, it is unlikely that they will want 'hands-on' responsibility within the business, but they may be prepared to act as a mentor. In fact they have a reason for doing so – part of their cash is tied up in your business. Many regions have thriving business angel communities, and it may be worth speaking to them early in the exit planning process. Perhaps they would be happy to give advice on raising funds, or other important matters. There is a caveat of course, which is that angels will be most interested in fast growing, profitable businesses that have an exciting future. They may not be too inspired if you approach them with a story along the lines of 'I have had enough and need to get out – let someone else take the hassle.' If this is your reason for developing an exit strategy, you need to polish up your PR a little. Chapter 5 may help you do this.

Contact details for the national UK body of business angels are provided in Appendix B.

Exchange of shares

When large businesses buy other similar sized organizations they often procure shares partly for cash, but with a further proportion paid by issuing shares to be held in the acquiring company. Sometimes money is not involved at all, with one type of share being exchanged for another at an agreed rate. There are all kinds of legal and financial implications of this type of arrangement, and professional advice is required if you are giving this approach any consideration.

A few general points are worth considering. First, if a publicly quoted plc is buying your firm (whose shares are tradable on the London Stock Exchange or another major stock market) and the offer is a straight share swap, to some extent the deal may be almost as good as cash. The acquiring company's shares can be openly sold via the stock market at a time of your choosing – although as the saying goes 'the value of shares can go up or down'. However, if your business is being bought by another private firm and you are offered shares in lieu of cash, it may be that you are transformed from a majority to a minority shareholder with all of the limitations this implies.

Remember Jack of 'beanstalk' fame? He swapped his mother's cow (which was her main business asset) for a bag of beans and all he achieved was an angry business partner and a furious ogre in the garden. Cash would have been a much more sensible option – his mother certainly thought so when she cuffed Jack around the ear. Ensure you don't become the angry ogre. Take professional advice to make certain you understand all of the implications.

The serial entrepreneur

When our serial entrepreneur sold his first business, he believed he had negotiated a good price. Furthermore, he expected the cash to be available in full at the time of completion. However, the buyer (who you will remember was a much larger competitor) wanted to structure payment around three (roughly equal) stages: one-third in cash on completion, a further third in cash after two years (in bank guaranteed loan notes to ensure the cash would be forthcoming), and a final third in shares of the acquiring company – which was a publicly floated plc. A limitation on the final 'third' of the payment meant that the shares could not be sold for two years. Although not as good as cash on signature, the deal nevertheless looked attractive and was duly completed. However, Tony was somewhat shocked when the first payment was made by cheque directly out of the company he had just sold. The first third was effectively his own money! He also realized that the second third would also come from profits the business made during the next two years, and the final third would be shares in the larger group. Effectively the buyer had bought Tony's business without needing cash, and it only occurred to him after he had signed his name. Tony was not too disappointed. He had become a wealthy man at a very young age and he got the last laugh. By the time he sold the shares in the parent company two years later, they had trebled in price. Even being bought with your own money can turn out right in the end!

One of the most satisfying aspects of being an entrepreneur is the ability to learn as you go. The next time our serial entrepreneur had reached the point where he wished to dispose of his business, he approached the funding aspect very differently. Realizing that a management buy out would allow him both to reward loyal employees and to provide a sensible exit route, he approached the businesses bankers directly. Essentially he persuaded the bank to provide the funding that would allow his employees to take over the business. Before doing so he market-tested the value of his business by entering into confidential discussions with competitors, to find out how much his business would be worth. Having secured this figure he was able to offer a 'discount' to his employees by agreeing to a smaller sum. This also impressed the bank, which was effectively lending against a business that had a higher value that the sale price. A win–win–win situation.

TAX PLANNING

Please note this serious disclaimer. The law surrounding taxation changes constantly. Before the last UK budget opposition parties and daily newspapers goaded the Chancellor of the Exchequer that he was planning to introduce his 100th new tax on 'hardworking families'. I don't wish to be party-political here; messing around with taxes is a favourite pastime of politicians from all walks of life. The purpose of this diatribe is to convince you to seek professional tax advice ahead of any decision to dispose of your business. The earlier you do so the better. I have included the next few paragraphs to help you think about which tax issues you should request detailed professional advice on in your situation. The consequences for failing to take proper tax advice early can be dire. Look on tax planning as an interesting intellectual activity rather than a chore or burden. John Maynard Keyes remarked that 'The avoidance of taxes is the only intellectual pursuit that still carries any reward.'

Capital gains tax (CGT)

When an asset is sold the basic principle of capital gains tax applies. The cost of acquiring the asset is subtracted from the disposal proceeds and the balance is defined as a capital gain. Don't be fooled if this sounds simple and appears easy to understand. Having calculated the capital gain you have to calculate the total tax payable by including (or deducting) allowances, costs, exempt amounts, reliefs and possibly other negative gains (known to you and me as losses). The specifics surrounding your particular situation may be very complicated, hence the need for professional advice.

One particular advantage of UK CGT rules at the time of writing is the opportunity to apply taper relief to the disposal of business assets under certain circumstances. Basically your business needs to be a qualifying company – the main qualification relates to it being a trading company, rather than, for example, being a 'holding company'. Speak to your accountant about this as if your business currently would not be 'qualified', it might well be in your interest to modify matters so that it becomes so.

If your company qualifies, the length of time that you have held shares becomes important. After one year the amount of CGT you pay will be halved, and after two years the sum is halved again. In essence, shares held in a qualifying company for two years would allow someone who would normally be liable to pay CGT at 40 per cent, to effectively pay only 10 per cent. (Perhaps you now understand why I suggest taking professional advice as soon as possible.)

Inheritance tax (IHT)

Inheritance tax does not just apply to property of value that is transferred on death. Gifts made during a person's lifetime can also be counted towards inheritance tax at the time of death, under certain circumstances. If you plan to pass on your business to members of your family (or even staff), you need to take expert advice on inheritance tax matters as soon as possible. As with most taxes, inheritance tax is subject to allowances, and under certain circumstances gifts might be tax-free. As a general rule, if you plan to pass on shares (or other assets) without charging the full market value, you need to survive seven years for the beneficiary to receive the full benefit of tax relief.

Activity: Preparing your own exit strategy

Hopefully, having read thus far, ideas have appeared inside your head relating to your business and how you might exit. This would be a good time to begin committing ideas to paper. If you wait until you have read through the whole book, some of the thoughts might have disappeared. Writing down your thoughts in a structured way has two benefits: ideas aren't lost and the writing process usually generates other thoughts and perhaps key questions, the answers to which will be crucial in successfully selling your business. At this stage don't worry too much about the structure of your strategy document, or about finding the precise wording. Just get something down on paper (or computer screen) and be prepared for your ideas to evolve as you work through the remainder of the book and beyond. For the moment I suggest you focus on six specific headings:

1. Objectives and aspirations.
2. Current valuation.
3. Opportunities for increasing the valuation.
4. Barriers to sale.
5. Sale process.
6. Tax planning.

1. Objectives and aspirations

Hopefully you began writing these down earlier. Take the opportunity to reflect on them again now. Perhaps you have not fully considered alternatives to selling your business, such as passing it onto your family, or spending less time working in it but still drawing a salary. Having too many possible exit routes is a problem, but it is a relatively nice problem. Take time to consider what is really important to you, your spouse and your family.

2. Current valuation

If you have not yet applied the various valuation methods to your business, do so now. Even if you can only produce rough estimates at this stage it will still assist.

3. Opportunities for increasing the valuation

Think about how you could increase the value of your business. Remember what was stated regarding the value that knowledge, ideas and relationships can bring. Doubling the value of your business does not necessarily require a doubling of customers, revenue or profit. It does require someone to multiply the value they put on your business by a factor of two.

4. Barriers to sale

There may be a number of barriers that will make it difficult to sell your business, or otherwise depress the valuation people place on it. As I have not explicitly covered these factors earlier it may be worth taking the time to do so here. First of all you need to apply the realism test. I hate to ask this, but is your business saleable in its current format? If it is a 'one man band', not profitable, has no long-term contracts and would not function without you, it is unlikely that a buyer will be forthcoming. (I say unlikely but not impossible – you may for example have a brilliant and unique idea that has value.) As much as I wish to encourage you to be positive on the subject of selling your business, we do exist in the real world. Assuming you have passed the realism test, what other factors might create impediments to a successful sale?

Other shareholders

If you are a minority shareholder you may find it difficult to sell the business unless you can persuade a majority that selling is a good idea. Even if you have a majority shareholding, minority shareholders can cause problems or scupper the deal. Much depends on what your shareholders' agreement says – should such a document exist at all. Some agreements affirm that minority shareholdings are automatically included in the sale if the majority of shareholders wish to sell. Lawyers often refer to these as 'drag and tag' rights. Ensure that other shareholders are supportive of your actions, or at least that they have to comply.

Poor record-keeping

Poor record-keeping and untidy files will cause you no end of difficulty, and could even prevent a profitable sale. If you consider this to be an over-statement, look ahead to Chapter 7, which focuses on legal documentation. When the due diligence process begins you will find yourself rapidly sinking beneath requests for information. If files are not in order you will have a very miserable experience.

Unsustainable profits

The importance of a broad customer base, contracted income and other factors were discussed in Chapter 2. If a potential buyer cannot clearly see how profits will be sustained in the longer term they are unlikely to be very interested. This ties in to the notion of creating the investment story. If there isn't one, you are unlikely to find a buyer.

Over-reliance on you

Unless you wish to sell some or all of your shares but remain within the business, you must structure key operations so that they function without your input. Many small businesses rely totally on the skills, enthusiasm and resources of the owner.

Problematic lease

Leases on property (or other assets) can be very onerous. In certain circumstances they can be a real impediment to a successful sale. From a planning perspective, if you have already signed a long-term lease that has very onerous clauses, you are stuck with it. However, if you need to renew a lease ahead of a planned sale it is worth considering how you might mitigate any potentially negative effects. Leases are considered in some detail in the 'retail' section of Chapter 8. Reading this will provide ideas that should be discussed with your legal adviser.

5. Sale process

Managing the sale process will be covered at length in Chapter 6, and other important factors are dealt with in future chapters. It is therefore perhaps unreasonable to ask you to map out your thoughts at this stage. However, it will be useful to begin thinking about some of the key topics now. Will you market the business yourself? Will you select a business broker? Will you rely on your current accountant or will you choose a firm with specialist experience?

6. Tax planning

Given the very limited advice contained within this book on the subject, I strongly suggest an early discussion with an accountant regarding both capital gains tax and inheritance tax. Planning ahead is one of the best strategies to minimizing your exposure.

Hopefully you now have a number of thoughts and ideas scrawled on a piece of paper, or lodged inside your computer's hard drive. Keep this information, however sketchy or badly constructed the ideas may appear. The rest of the book aims to help you refine and develop your approach into one that will maximize your chances for a profitable sale.

Chapter summary

▐ Planning ahead is crucial if you want to maximize control and value.
▐ Set your parameters for success. Does this involve great wealth or a modest lump sum? Factor in other things – not just money.
▐ Create realistic timescales.
▐ Target potential buyers early. Learn to influence them (see Chapter 5 for ideas).
▐ Manage how you exit. Will it be important to take cash and leave immediately, or would a lock-in situation suit you?
▐ Take expert advice to help you minimize tax payable.
▐ Think carefully about barriers to entry. They will not be insurmountable if considered early enough.

4

Professional Advisers

'All professions are a conspiracy against the laity.' So said George Bernard Shaw in the first half of the 20th century. Had he been a 21st-century business owner he may have had reason to modify his views somewhat. To balance Shaw's quote, consider this little nugget offered by the celebrity fire-fighter Red Adair: 'If you think hiring a professional is expensive, try hiring an amateur.' The 21st century is a complex and litigious era in which to exist, and selling something as important and valuable as a business requires professionalism and specialist knowledge – at least in parts. This chapter deals with hiring and managing professionals.

Choosing the most appropriate professional advisers – and managing them in the correct way – will help you achieve a better sale price for your business, and ensure you keep more of the proceeds. Note that I specifically refer to 'managing' your professional advisers. It seems to me that most people, whether in business or in private life, make no effort to retain control when they employ a 'professional'. People appear to leave their own skills, ideas and experience at the door of their accountant or solicitor (or doctor and dentist for that matter). Why is this? There could be a whole range of reasons. Perhaps historical factors play a key role? A hundred years ago the only people with a degree and a 'professional education' in your locality would be the doctor, the lawyer and the priest. Oh, and if you were lucky the local schoolmaster. All of these would almost certainly be men. Unless you were the local squire or had significant private means, an unlettered person like yourself could expect a short interview with one of the educated professionals before they pronounced the course of action. All you had to do was touch your forelock and pay their fees – in guineas, of course.

Times have changed, but people in the traditional professions always seem to cling to the past longer than the rest of us. It was only during the mid-1980s that the Law Society allowed solicitors to advertise. Imagine that. You study for five years and then set up in business but can't tell anyone! And we were expected to rely on these people to keep us out of prison or the bankruptcy court. Nevertheless, modern accountants and lawyers are a much more commercial breed than their forebears and in the competitive modern environment, are falling over themselves to help your business. The extent to which they help in the sale of your business lies in your hands. This chapter offers ideas on choosing and managing professional advisers.

ACCOUNTANTS

An experienced accountant can add immeasurable value by assisting in the preparatory work ahead of a sale. First of all, as we discovered in Chapter 2, an experienced accountant may be far better placed to provide advice on valuing your business than most other types of adviser. A medium-sized accountancy firm will have clients across many sectors and will have been exposed to the process of buying and selling companies. In addition to having a view on the relevant 'multiple' that your business may be worth, accountants have experience in (legally) manipulating profit and loss accounts and balance sheets to ensure the maximum figure is represented. As we noted earlier, it is logical that if you value your business by the 'multiple' method, maximizing the profit figure to be multiplied is a very sensible place to start.

Should you use your existing accountant to advise on a business sale?

The answer to this question, as with many others, is that it depends. It might depend on the size of the sale, or the financial complexity of the deal. It might depend on the size and depth of experience within the firm of accountants that you use. It might also depend on the relationship you have with your accountant.

Employing an experienced and motivated accountant can help you prepare your business for sale, and minimize taxation. The kind of question you should be asking yourself will revolve around whether your accountant has:

▍ Recent experience in advising on planning ahead for the successful sale of businesses of a similar size to yours. This experience would include issues such as tax planning and inheritance planning.

▊ Recent experience in advising through a business sale process, cover-
ing issues such as liaising with HMRC for tax clearances.
▊ Contacts who may be interested in buying your business or helping to
find a buyer.
▊ Innovative ideas that generate options for you.
▊ The resources to work to your timescales.

To put the above into context, here a few examples of the type of issues/
questions that I have in mind.

Maybe you have a retail business and own the freehold on the property.
Would it be more advantageous to try to sell the business and property
separately? Should you retain the property and lease it to the new business
owner? Are their any tax implications of the different approaches? If you
keep and lease the property, what would be the impact on your personal
taxation in retirement? Could you put the property into a pension?

Perhaps you run a business and your daughter is a minority shareholder.
Do you wish to maximize the money that she gets from the sale? If so,
should she buy further shares ahead of time? Should you reallocate shares
as A and B type?

The answers to these questions can be very important. They can affect
how you sell and help you plan ahead. Frankly, if you don't start asking
questions, by the time anyone else mentions them it may be too late. The
world of taxation is a very complex one, and some aspects are extremely
counter-intuitive. I learnt a painful and salutary lesson many years ago.
I had been a partner/investor in a small business that I didn't physically
work in. After a couple of years my other business interests took over and
I decided to pull out of the venture. My business partner bought out my
interest, and I was able to reclaim my capital investment. Despite the fact
that I had made no profit and had taken no salary or other form of drawing,
I found myself paying income tax on non-existent earnings! How can you
be taxed on no money? I couldn't believe this was possible, but it was. I
can't remember the details and it will be too painful to trawl through my
records. Never assume you understand the financial implications of any
action relating to the sale of your business without taking professional
advice from an accountant.

In researching this chapter I spoke to a number of accountants who
specialize in the area of corporate finance and therefore spend most of
their working lives advising on the sale and acquisition of businesses.
What advice would a specialist accountant give to a business owner
considering selling up?

The first piece of advice proffered by everyone is 'Think ahead.' This is quickly followed by 'Plan ahead.' Why plan ahead? Because you may be able to bolster profits, minimize corporation tax, reduce capital gains tax, or create a more compelling story for potential buyers to latch on to. Put simply, planning ahead can affect the cash you are left with. It will not surprise many readers to learn that the next piece of professional advice involves 'selecting an accountant with appropriate experience'. This is useful advice and little more needs to be said on this subject. If you needed hip replacement surgery you wouldn't approach a cardiac surgeon would you?

How an accountant can help

There are basically five ways in which an accountant may be able to assist:

1. Help assess the optimum value of your business.
2. Advise on factors that will influence how much of the cash you get to keep.
3. Help find a buyer (and pre-qualify them as a serious bidder rather than a 'tyre kicker').
4. Advise on financial matters as the sale proceeds.
5. Advise on investment opportunities following the sale.

All of these factors warrant detailed consideration.

1. Putting the optimum value on your business

If you have chosen an appropriately experienced accountant, he or she will have handled many business disposals across a range of sectors, hopefully including the one your business operates in. He or she will also know where to look to find broader evidence of the 'multiple' (see Chapter 2) that has historically been applied to businesses like yours. Your accountant should also be aware of any local factors that might affect the price, and of course have a network of contacts with similar experience that he or she can speak to. An accountant can examine your balance sheet and profit and loss account and advise how to move things around in a way that will increase value.

2. Maximizing the cash that you eventually keep

Selling your business will cost money. You will have to pay professional fees (discussed later in this chapter) and will also suffer a number of indirect costs involved in generating information, attending meetings and so on. However, all of theses costs are likely to be dwarfed by the cost of paying taxation – the government wants a piece of the action too. There are still a number of lawful means of reducing taxation and an accountant is best placed to advise. Some of the advice might be radical ('go and live abroad') and some simple but effective. As the law on taxation consistently changes (and I don't really understand it anyway) I have decided not to include any tax advice in this book in case you are reading it three years from now and everything is out of date. Don't skimp on paying for advice that will help reduce the tax burden.

3. Finding a buyer

It shouldn't surprise you to learn that in general accountants get to know a lot of people who, a) run businesses and, b) have enough money to need an accountant. There is a more than reasonable chance that the person (or business) that buys your shares will come from one of these groups. It therefore makes sense to speak to an accountant who may be in a position to identify a potential buyer from within his or her network (and that network's network).

   Not only can an accountant potentially help with networking, but he or she can also assist by producing documentation that will generate interest. The term for this document is the 'sale memorandum'. The purpose of the sale memorandum is to provide information about your business in a format that makes potential buyers want to find out more. This will include providing an overview of the business, its assets, customer base, history and prospects. It will be a combination of headline financial information and a story about how the business makes money and why it will do so in the future. You could of course produce the sale memorandum yourself, but having an experienced accountant do this on your behalf has two benefits. First, he or she has done so on numerous occasions so will probably produce a more professional document, and secondly, he or she can ensure the document is issued confidentially. It should be possible to create a sales memorandum on a 'no name disclosed' basis that would be difficult to identify with your business. Obviously at some point the interested party would be advised of the name of your business, but not before their interest level (and perhaps resources) had been tested and they have signed a confidentiality agreement. Advice on preparing a sale memorandum is provided in Chapter 7.

4. Advise on financial matters as the sale proceeds

Unless your business sale involves very small sums or is extremely simple, the buyer will have an accountant completing a financial due diligence process. This may well generate questions and requests for information that are not straightforward, and you will benefit from the support of an accountant in providing appropriate responses. Chapter 7 on legal documentation covers the due diligence process in detail.

5. Advise on investment opportunities

You used to have a business but now you have cash. Hopefully most of it will remain intact even after paying professional advisers and putting a chunk aside for tax. What will you do with it? Do you have well-developed investment plans? There are plenty of people who would like to advise you on 'excellent' investment opportunities, including your bank, which will have spotted the large amount of money that just entered your account. You accountant will (hopefully) be the source of 'independent' advice, and if he or she works in a medium-sized practice may even have colleagues who specialize in investments.

LAWYERS

Whatever the size and value of your business, you will almost certainly require the services of a solicitor during the sale process. Chapter 7 deals with the complex area of legal contracts, but for now I need to draw attention to a range of factors that will help when selecting and appointing a solicitor.

Why you require a solicitor

Almost all transactions that we enter into, in both our private and business lives, involve entering into contracts covered by law. Most contracts are fairly small in importance, and informal in structure. If you call into the local newsagent and buy a newspaper (or any other product), you have entered into a contract. The same applies if you buy petrol, a meal in a restaurant or theatre tickets, or have a drink in your local pub.

One significant aspect of contract law relates to whether the transaction involves private individuals or companies. The law offers significant protection to private individuals, especially when they are buying from large organizations. Statutory laws such as the Consumer Credit Acts and Sale of Good Acts offer legal remedies in the event that you are mislead or supplied with defective products. Significantly less protection is offered when two organizations enter into contractual relationships. In this scenario the law takes the view that you have jointly agreed to an arrangement that meets the needs of both parties. Unless there are extenuating circumstances (such as clear evidence of misrepresentation by one party) the contract will generally be considered binding in its present form. If you have ever examined a detailed commercial contract you will know that every term is tied down to a specific meaning – a device used by lawyers to ensure that the scope for interpreting the contract in different ways is minimized. The general rule is that when you sign a contract you are agreeing to all of its clauses – and the rights and responsibilities contained within them. I am not qualified to offer legal advice to readers or even to myself, so the best suggestion I have is *involve a solicitor* when entering into contractual negotiations with your prospective purchaser.

Which solicitor?

Solicitors tend to specialize in different aspects of the law. In most countries, laws have evolved over hundreds of years, and in England and Wales we are bound by historical case laws, laws made by Parliament, laws created via the European Union, and even local by-laws and regulations. It is not surprising that no single solicitor can offer genuine expertise in all aspects of the law. Law firms counter this by having a range of specialists within the organization so that they can offer a broad range of services. In my city there are dozens of solicitors firms and most of them cover the key legal disciplines required by the local population, including conveyancing of property, preparation of wills, divorce and criminal law. However, not all of them can offer significant experience in more commercial aspects of law – which includes advice on the preparation of business-sale contracts.

The first business I owned was a 'partnership'. Another person and I owned the business in equal shares and we asked our 'generalist' local solicitor to draw up a partnership agreement. This worked very well. Later we founded a business that was incorporated as a limited company. However, when the time came to sell this business our generalist local solicitor suggested we employ a commercial specialist, as his experience in this aspect of law was limited. I consider this excellent advice. He turned the work down because he considered other law firms could offer better experience/service. He even suggested a number of firms – and lawyers within them – that might be suited to our requirements. The solicitor that we eventually instructed had spent most of his professional life advising medium-sized local firms and helped in the preparation of business sale contracts many times each year. Not only could he provide excellent legal advice, he also had suggestions on other practical matters involved in selling a business.

Host a beauty parade

When large businesses are sold (which involve very high transaction costs) it is common for the seller to hold a kind of 'beauty parade' in deciding which firm of solicitors to employ. Basically this involves assessing a number of different firms to identify which one offers the best 'fit' and also the greatest overall value. If you are selling a small business it may be over the top and impractical to do this. However, one good piece of advice is to speak to two or three solicitors before deciding which one to proceed with. Almost all solicitors will be happy to have an initial meeting free of charge, and this obviously gives them the chance to understand the scope of the project, and consider how attractive it is to them (ensure they agree ahead of the initial meeting that it will be free and without obligation).

How will you judge which firm is best for you? You could go on 'gut instinct' and this isn't necessarily a bad approach. After all you are looking to select a firm (or really an individual within that firm) that you feel comfortable dealing with. It may be useful, however, to try and set the criteria that will be most important to you ahead of the initial meeting, to bring a little structure and impartiality into the process.

Checklist for selecting a law firm

☐ Does it have a specialist 'commercial lawyer' or commercial department? (You should be meeting someone from that department.)

☐ Can it demonstrate that it undertakes many business transactions each year?

☐ Can it demonstrate experience of handling transactions of a similar size to yours?

☐ Does it have experience in your business sector?

☐ Who would manage the process on its behalf? (Ideally, the person you are dealing with. One of the potential problems in employing professional services firms is that you initially

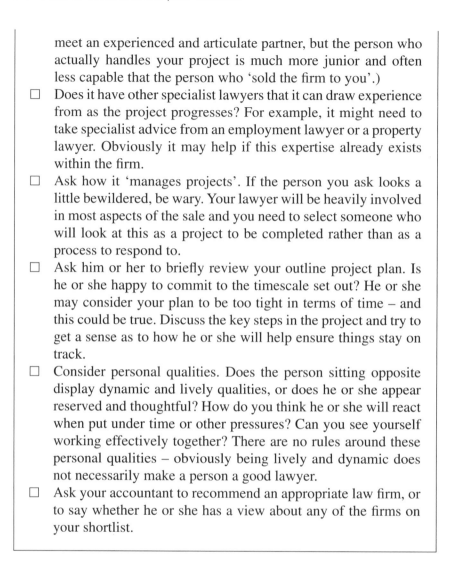

meet an experienced and articulate partner, but the person who actually handles your project is much more junior and often less capable that the person who 'sold the firm to you'.)

☐ Does it have other specialist lawyers that it can draw experience from as the project progresses? For example, it might need to take specialist advice from an employment lawyer or a property lawyer. Obviously it may help if this expertise already exists within the firm.

☐ Ask how it 'manages projects'. If the person you ask looks a little bewildered, be wary. Your lawyer will be heavily involved in most aspects of the sale and you need to select someone who will look at this as a project to be completed rather than as a process to respond to.

☐ Ask him or her to briefly review your outline project plan. Is he or she happy to commit to the timescale set out? He or she may consider your plan to be too tight in terms of time – and this could be true. Discuss the key steps in the project and try to get a sense as to how he or she will help ensure things stay on track.

☐ Consider personal qualities. Does the person sitting opposite display dynamic and lively qualities, or does he or she appear reserved and thoughtful? How do you think he or she will react when put under time or other pressures? Can you see yourself working effectively together? There are no rules around these personal qualities – obviously being lively and dynamic does not necessarily make a person a good lawyer.

☐ Ask your accountant to recommend an appropriate law firm, or to say whether he or she has a view about any of the firms on your shortlist.

So selecting an appropriate lawyer is not really a question of reaching for the *Yellow Pages* and picking the first firm that catches your eye. Nor is it about finding the cheapest quote. It is about finding someone with appropriate experience that you feel would best represent your interests, who you could work with.

The lawyer's view

I spoke at length with an experienced commercial lawyer, with the objective of understanding how a lawyer sees the value that they bring to the process. The person I talked to has handled numerous business transactions, assisting both buyers and sellers in many sectors. What advice would he offer to someone selling a business when selecting an appropriately qualified commercial lawyer?

'Overall the objective of the legal adviser is to ensure the deal is completed in a manner that means the client can sign the documents, put them in a drawer and then sleep at night. The buyer's legal advisers will be looking for formal warranties and indemnities to cover all eventualities – effectively to minimize their client's risk at the expense of the seller. The role of the seller's lawyer is to ensure that risk is quantified and minimized, without spoiling the deal. Achieving this not only requires legal skills, but also commercial judgement, which is only developed through extensive experience. In many situations the commercial lawyer also acts as project manager, pulling together specialist advice and liaising with the client's financial advisers and professional advisers representing the buyer. Managing this process effectively requires a much broader range of skills than merely interpreting contract and commercial law. My advice would be to find a law firm with extensive experience in helping clients in both buying and selling businesses, that can demonstrate a broad and deep understanding of how businesses operate. It might also be useful to ensure your lawyer has a few grey hairs – he or she has probably earned them through constant involvement in challenging contractual situations!'

I asked how he markets his practice – how he aims to differentiate himself from other law firms and demonstrate the skills and expertise set out above. 'Much of our work comes from referrals. Our objective is not merely to earn a fee, but to develop a relationship. We are here to serve the client, and when they are happy they tell others. We also ensure that we are active in the business community. This is not just about networking, but ensuring we understand how businesses are operating in our region – understanding the specific issues and challenges they face. This is all part of developing the commercial experience and judgement that I mentioned earlier.

My summary suggestion is that when selling a business, take time to identify the best legal firm to support you – one that has the right people and experience. Getting this right can be important through-out the sale process and beyond.'

Paying legal fees

Let's assume that you have approached a small number of firms and have identified the best one to support you. How much will it cost? Obviously that depends on the size and scope of the deal. It also depends on the size and location of the firm that you choose. If you live in London or another major city, and employ one of the larger firms working out of plush central offices, you will pay for it. But there is a balance to be struck here, because if you choose a very small out-of-town firm it may be significantly cheaper, but does it have the resources and experience? Perhaps the best advice is to approach whichever firm seems most appropriate and then assess it against the criteria set out above. Having done this ask for an estimate of the total cost of the project – and also enquire whether the firm would be happy to work for a fixed fee. Generally speaking, it should be possible for it to provide a fixed-fee approach – especially if it has significant experience in this type of work.

One small word of caution: having a fixed-fee arrangement will not guarantee there will be no extras to pay. Your lawyer will probably agree to a fixed fee on the basis of 'the deal proceeding in accordance with expectations'. You may consider that the statement gives them quite a broad range of 'get-outs'. After all, whose expectations are we talking about? Ensure it is made clear that should additional costs become likely you are advised immediately – not at the end of the project. Nasty surprises are not in the interest of either party.

BUSINESS BROKERS

The third category of professional adviser may be one that you are less familiar with. In fact, I am not even sure what to call them. They are known as 'business sale agents', 'business brokers', 'business transfer agents', 'business valuation agents' or a host of other similar names. For simplicity, I will refer to them as 'business brokers', although in picking a single term I have to acknowledge that I might be doing some of them a disservice, as they don't all necessarily do the same things. If you type the words 'business broker' (or any of the other terms listed) into a search engine you should be presented with a wide range of firms, all claiming to offer an excellent service in helping you sell your business. You will quickly find that some organizations appear to specialize in certain sectors – for example focusing on property-based businesses such as pubs or post offices. Others appear to deal mainly with retail-service type businesses such as hairdressers or beauty salons. If you think it might be appropriate to use the services of a business broker, a key challenge is to find the one best suited to your needs. More on this later.

Who needs a business broker?

Would it be appropriate for you to employ the services of a business broker? Should you pursue this approach rather than managing things yourself with the help of an accountant and solicitor? Of course the answer is that it depends. Employing the services of a business broker should mean less work for you, and where you have to complete tasks they will be able to help ensure you do the right things at the right time. An experienced broker will have helped many businesses go through exactly the process you will have to navigate, and therefore can be of invaluable assistance. But couldn't an experienced accountant also offer such support? In answering this question it may be helpful to consider the key things that a business broker offers.

Advice on preparing your business for sale

An experienced business broker should be in a position to advise on how to prepare your business for sale. But will they be any better placed to understand you business than your accountant, who probably has quite a detailed knowledge of how your business functions?

Preparing the sale memorandum

The sale memorandum is a structured document used as an aid to marketing. It describes your business in detail with a view to generating interest in prospective purchasers. It is feasible to create the document yourself, and how to do so is explored in Chapter 5. However, it is quite common for an accountancy firm to produce the document on your behalf as it is more experienced at handling financial aspects. Also, having financial projections validated by a firm of accountants may lend credibility (even though projections can rarely be more than 'best guesses'). Most business brokers also offer to create the sale memorandum on your behalf, and if they have appropriate financial expertise, may produce an equally good job. Ideas for evaluating the relative expertise of the business broker in this regard are given below.

Valuing your business

Most business brokers will help you put a valuation on your business. Hopefully, by this stage in the book you will be wary of anyone who claims to know exactly how much your business is worth. As we know, it depends on what valuation method is employed and also a range of other factors such as what multiple is used or how profits are measured. Where good business brokers could add value is if they have genuine and recent experience of selling a similar business in your sector (or geographical area). Ask them directly if they have examples.

Finance

Many business brokers claim to be able to help raise finance through links they have with banks and investment institutions. Obviously it makes sense that they have developed relationships with providers of finance as presumably they generate a lot of business. If raising finance might ordinarily be tricky in your particular situation, there may be an advantage to at least entering discussions with a business broker. However, you ought to bear in mind that they may well have commercial relationships of their own with finance providers and may not be providing impartial advice.

Links with other professionals

Business brokers will also have links with law firms and accountants that they can recommend. On the plus side it ought to be taken for granted that they recommend experienced and qualified professional advisers. However, the problem of independence raises it head again. Are they recommending the most appropriate firms, or their friends? Are they making a margin on passing through your business (which is obviously charged to you in some form or other)?

Marketing

A key claim of many business brokers is that they have access to potential buyers and have methods for generating interest in your business. This ought to be true, after all it is probably the most important part of their function. If you trawl through a number of websites it will become clear to you that some agents do little more than provide an internet listing. Others offer both internet listings plus an insertion in a magazine, and most offer to create 'particulars' in the way that an estate agent does in respect of a house sale. A few firms found on the internet offer direct marketing solutions – they will actively contact people and generally attempt to promote your business. This may well be the most successful approach, but of course it costs money. This really brings us to the key question: if you choose to use a business broker, how do you find the one that's right for you?

Selecting a business broker

If you conduct an internet search and examine the websites of a number of business brokers you will find lots of similarities. They more or less all claim to be good at the same things: helping you prepare for the sale, creating an accurate valuation, accessing potential buyers and so on. How on earth are you expected to choose the firm that's right for you? I'm afraid the short answer involves the most work. You have to invest time in finding out what these firms are really like. The way to do this involves asking lots of questions and then listening carefully to the answers. As a general rule I suggest you ask for hard evidence to support any claims they make. The best firms will have little difficulty in providing it. Here are some examples that might be of assistance:

Claim: 'We will prepare a detailed and professionally presented sale memorandum.'
Evidence: 'Please provide me with three examples of the sale memoranda you have created for others.'
Claim: 'We have extensive experience in your sector.'
Evidence: 'Please provide details of the last three similar businesses that you successfully sold.'
Claim: 'We can provide an accurate valuation of your business.'
Evidence: 'Provide a written description of the process and methodology you will use. Confirm how you know the correct multiple that might be applicable to my specific business.'
Claim: 'We have helped to sell hundreds of businesses for satisfied clients.'
Evidence: 'Please provide a list of at least 10 clients I can call to ask about the service they received.' (Ensure you do this; do not just accept pre-written client testimonials.)

You might think that this approach involves a lot of effort, but unless someone you know and trust can recommend a specific business broker, how can you identify the one that will work hardest on your behalf? You might only sell a business once, so it is worth investing time in ensuring that any assistance you pay for is the best available.

Chapter summary

▮ Professional advisers 'advise'. It remains your job to manage them effectively.

▮ Chose an accountant with experience in handling business disposals.

▮ Accountants can help assess the value of a business and prepare financial data to validate the valuation.

▮ Consider using an accountant to create the sale memorandum. Can you exploit the commercial contacts of your chosen accountant?

▮ You will require the services of a solicitor – unless your business is very small and simple you should select a specialist commercial lawyer.

▮ Take time to select individuals who you can work with.

▮ Always negotiate professional fees. Aim to achieve a capped or fixed fee.

▮ Business brokers provide more formal sales channels than many accountancy or legal firms.

▮ Many brokers specialize in certain sectors – for example post offices or pubs.

▮ There are many brokers offering services – find them using the internet.

▮ Business brokers aren't formally regulated by statutory professional bodies, unlike accountants or lawyers. This means you have to work a little harder to ensure your chosen broker is as good as its promotional materials suggest.

▮ Brokers charge a broad range of fees. Perhaps you get what you pay for. Consider agreeing a success-based fee. The more you pay up front, the less they need to sell your business.

5

Marketing Your Business

'Half of the money I spend on advertising is wasted – the trouble is, I don't know which half.' This saying is attributed to John Wanamaker, who was a department store owner in the United States in the 1870s. In today's much more complex and sophisticated environment, it remains a truism that a sizeable proportion of all marketing expenditure is wasted, but nobody can really predict or abolish the waste. Think of all the junk mail that drops through your letterbox en route to your recycling bin.

What is even more wasteful than badly targeted marketing is developing a good business that is never profitably sold because of *inadequate or ill-considered marketing activity*. Put another way, no one will buy your business if they don't know of its existence. Becoming known isn't difficult. What takes slightly more care is becoming well-known for positive reasons, in other words, having a strong *reputation*. It may occur to you that reputations are not made overnight and a key message in this chapter will be to create a structured approach to developing the profile and reputation that your business enjoys. Why put time and effort into this activity? Solid business reasons: what potential buyers think about your business will impact the amount they are willing to pay.

Although this book focuses on smaller businesses, the principles on which all businesses are valued remain the same. We can gain valuable insights into the type of factors that will positively affect people's perception of the value of a business by glancing at what the financial press has to say about larger organizations.

Here is a random sample of reasons that share-tipsters and financial journalists gave for recommending specific shares, all taken from the financial press over just a few days:

▌ A telecoms firm is 'achieving strong growth'.

■ A training firm showed a 'rise in operating profits'.
■ A food production firm is subject to 'bid speculation' (as was a transport business, a storage company and a retailer).
■ A confectionery firm is producing 'healthy snack bars'.
■ A web services company has '34 FTSE 100 clients'.
■ A finance firm 'should do well in the current market turbulence'.
■ A storage business 'should expand significantly'.
■ A house builder had a 'valuable land bank'.
■ A security firm 'reorganized and improved focus'.
■ A steel fabricator 'should do well in the run-up to the London 2012 Olympics'.
■ Three businesses were considered to be undervalued simply because they have 'low p/e ratios' (see Chapter 2 to be reminded of the p/e valuation method).

For the sake of balance I should also note that many shares were recommended as 'sells' rather than 'buys'. The reasons given were equally intriguing:

■ An orange grower faced 'global market volatility'.
■ A chemical company 'looks to be in real trouble'.
■ A computer firm had 'a dearth of ideas to rejuvenate the firm'.
■ A retailer had 'poor sales'.
■ A media business was 'vulnerable to rising costs'.
■ An IT business had 'lost key staff'.

(The fact that newspapers and magazines perceive many more reasons to 'buy' rather than 'sell' suggests the triumph of hope over caution. However, this is good news from a seller's perspective.)

This brief snapshot provides a fascinating insight into the factors that positively (and negatively) impact people's perceptions about businesses – and the fact that perceptions can be turned into some kind of financial value. If potential buyers believe that your business is 'achieving strong growth' or has an 'impressive client base', their perception of value will increase. You may have noticed that some of the reasons given don't relate to past performance but to expected future enhancements: 'should expand significantly', 'should do well', 'reorganized and improved focus'. You can be given credit for improving your focus! Therefore, what people think of your business is financially important.

PUBLIC RELATIONS

The first topic in this chapter on marketing will therefore deal with 'public relations' (PR). What is PR? PR is the way you manage your firms' reputation. In other words, managing what others think about your business with specific reference (in this case) to factors that will support a positive valuation. PR has two objectives: to tell people your business exists and to make them feel positive about it. Larger organizations usually have a whole department focused on this singular activity. The PR team will often be a subset of the marketing department, whose primary focus in life often appears to be to build a 'brand'. Brands are strange things. They are unquestionably real, but very difficult to define, touch or even visualize. Perhaps a key element of all brands concerns recognition. This relates to the ideas that occur in people's heads when they hear your company name or see its logo. I am no expert on brand management, and this book isn't the place to discuss the subject in detail anyway, but two points are important. First, if you can develop a unique and recognizable brand (for positive reasons) this may be the most valuable asset your business has. Think of Coca-Cola, for example. Are its greatest assets the bottling plants or lorries that deliver to shops, pubs and supermarkets? I doubt it. Its greatest asset is the brand name, which is known literally throughout the world. The second key point is that brand names, and the values they imply, must reflect reality. After all 'brand' isn't just about logos and registered trade marks; it is about how your business does things. Do the claims made of behalf of your business collapse when tested by reality? Does your brand (and PR materials) proclaim 'we care', but in reality you have an appalling record in failing to satisfactorily handle customer complaints? (Remember what I said earlier about selling a business requiring ruthless objectivity.) If your brand, and PR efforts on behalf of the brand, doesn't reflect reality, you will be storing up huge problems. Enough of the sophisticated stuff. Back to PR.

You may feel that PR will be expensive, and if you pay others to do it on your behalf you may well be right. Most PR firms I have visited have offices in expensive locations, costly furnishings and a car park full of German vehicles. Someone is paying for this and logic suggests it is the clients. But there is a great deal that you can do yourself – a kind of DIY approach to PR. The trade press in almost all business sectors are hungry for stories to fill their pages. If you approach them correctly they will be happy to print stories about you. However, before we get to the mechanics of getting into print, it is important to focus on *whom* you wish to target your PR efforts towards and what messages you might give to influence them.

Identifying your target audience

In Chapter 1 we asked, 'Who will buy your business?' Hopefully you got the message that buyers could emerge from a broad range of groups, including competitors, customers, employees and suppliers. However, in identifying your PR audience it pays to think more broadly still. Remember Ray in Chapter 3, who sold his print business through his physiotherapist? Does this suggest that it might be important for non-business-related acquaintances to know at least a little about the company that you run? When selling a small business you just never know who might help you find a buyer, or be a buyer themselves. Here are suggestions as to which groups might make up your target PR audience, and you may be able to think of others:

- customers;
- potential customers;
- competitors;
- investors, shareholders or your bank;
- suppliers;
- staff;
- professional advisers;
- family, friends and neighbours;
- non-business acquaintances (your physiotherapist!);
- local business community;
- local residential community;
- regulatory and other government bodies;
- the media (local or national press, industry journals).

Clearly the relative importance of each group will depend on the type of business you operate. If you run a sandwich shop it is likely that a potential buyer will be found in a relatively small geographical boundary, close to your business. It is also the type of business that 'first-time buyers' may be attracted to. (They may think 'I could do that.') Focusing PR on the local business and residential community, along with family friends and neighbours, could make a lot of sense. However, if you run a specialist engineering consultancy that works globally it is unlikely that your buyer will be very local. (You may, however, wish to communicate with your local community for other reasons – perhaps to establish your 'green credentials'.) Back in Chapter 1 I suggested that you write a list of all the potential buyers of your business, and hopefully you will have added to it since. Dig out the list and complete the following exercise.

Activity: Identify your PR audience

Using the list above, consider your target PR audience from the perspective of what kind of firm or person may be interested in buying your business. Don't allow yourself to think too narrowly at this stage (you can always discount things later). When you have a list of reasonable length, prioritize it in terms of which groups (or individuals) are most likely to be interested in acquiring your business, and could muster the resources to do so. Put those with highest priority at the top. This will help you think through the best kind of messages and media that could be employed, and will be helpful in working through the next sections.

Reaching your target audience

Now that you have identified and prioritized your target audience we can examine a range of PR techniques that can get you noticed in a positive way. Some methods will be more appropriate than others in your specific circumstances, but try not to discount any approach until you have considered the opportunities carefully.

Press releases

Press releases are an effective method of getting your message across. It is possible for this process to be effective at a local level, on an industry-specific level and (if your releases are newsworthy enough) at a national level. First of all you should recognize that all publishers of newspapers or magazines have a problem: filling their pages with interesting items. Both newspapers and industry journals carry a lot of news, so why not give them some? You may be thinking that you don't have anything newsworthy, but think again. To encourage your creative juices, the following is a list of newsworthy subjects that were published in two trade journals that I selected at random:

- new product launch;
- new investment in machinery;
- new business acquisition;
- new website/podcast;
- new business name/branding;
- successful court case;
- new software selected;

- services outsourced to a third-party provider;
- charitable donation;
- interesting statistics (more on this later);
- green issues (tree planting);
- new appointments (dozens of them);
- new prize (more on this later, too);
- new strategic direction;
- office move;
- 100th customer;
- the effect of interest rates.

Try it. Pick up any journal or trade publication and you will be staggered at the range of stories they are happy to print. (I also found a range of negative stories, usually involving the word 'receivership', but if you have attracted the attention of the press for this reason the book has arrived too late.) Notice how many stories involve the word 'new' (well, where do you think the term 'news' comes from?) When my business was just getting off the ground I decided that raising our profile with customers, competitors and suppliers would be useful. Each time we won a new piece of business (or in fact did almost anything – even when we moved office) I drafted a press release and sent it to the two main trade journals in our sector. Not only did they print stories, but journalists rang us up and asked impertinent questions (such as, 'How much is the new contract worth?') and requested digital photos.

You should not find it difficult to get press releases published, but there are some simple rules that will help ensure that publishers become interested in what you have to say. The first rule is that your news should be, well, new. If your press release advises that you acquired a customer six months ago it probably will not be worth publishing. Of course you don't have to tell them it was six months ago. This doesn't mean lying, just be careful with your words. For example, your release could begin with the phrase, 'Mugging's Engineering Limited today announced the successful signing of a major supply contract with Treetop Construction.' Notice the kind of words I have used: 'today', 'announced', 'successful' and 'major'. All positive 'success' words that suggest something important has happened. Other strong words include 'deal', 'completion', 'event', 'milestone', 'exciting' and 'award'. The list is endless. You don't require much writing talent or even exceptional news – just a well-structured and brief document that includes carefully chosen words and phrases. You may find that the following example generates ideas in your own mind about possible uses of the press release for your business. If so, write them down immediately.

Here's an example of a press release.

Biggins Sandwich Shop
High Street, Leftbury

PRESS RELEASE
1 February 2008

Leftbury Fast Food Supplier Scores Top Marks in Hygiene Inspection

Just 12 months after opening on Leftbury High Street, Biggins Sandwich Shop today announced it has scored an amazing 100 per cent during the annual hygiene inspection carried out by environmental health officers. Joe Biggins, who owns and personally runs the business said 'We are thrilled. We take every possible care with our hygiene practices and it is fantastic that the council's environmental health professionals appreciate all our hard work.' He added 'Producing great food is not just about the freshest and highest quality ingredients; a spotlessly clean environment is essential too.'

For more information contact:
Joe Biggins on 0000 0000 0000
Leftbury Environmental Services Department can be contacted on 0000 0000 0000.

Simple and a little cheesy? Maybe, but a local newspaper would run the story and on a quiet news week Joe Biggins may find that a journalist and photographer call around for a chat and a sandwich.

As short and simple as this release may be, it contains a number of elements you would do well to make note of. First, it is headed 'press release', so when it hits the desk/fax/e-mail address of the news editor they will know what it is (don't make them guess). Another important point is the date – confirming the 'new' element. Also notice contact numbers are given 'for more information'. Make it easy for the recipient to contact you. If they have to search for the number, the release may get put aside. Also notice the use of a quotation. News editors love quotes. Another point to note is that this remains a local story. It would be of interest to the local newspaper but would be unlikely to attract national attention. Therefore the local council is mentioned, and a contact number is shown for the environmental health department.

I hope you spotted the success words: 'top marks', 'amazing', '100 per cent', 'thrilled', 'fantastic', 'hard work', 'great food', 'highest quality', 'spotlessly clean' and 'essential'. You may feel uncomfortable using these success words about yourself or your business; after all isn't modesty a virtue? In business it is not a virtue and if my sandwich shop scored top marks in a hygiene review I would shout it from the rooftops. If I had plans to sell the business in the not too distant future I would take the time to shout louder and longer. Remember, what people think about your business will significantly affect their interest level, and how much they consider it to be worth.

A press release template is included in Appendix A. Have it in front of you whilst completing the following activity.

Activity: Draft a press release

Think of something that has happened in your business recently. A new contract award or perhaps a newly appointed employee (look back over previous pages and review the list of articles found in two trade journals for ideas).

Using the press release template begin to draft out your release. Ensure you communicate:

▪ who you are;
▪ where you are;
▪ what you have done;
▪ when it happened (now, today, etc);
▪ why it is important.

Try to keep it on one page and remember to use 'success' words. Ensure your contact details are prominent.

Now think about who you would send it to. A local newspaper? A trade journal? You may even consider local radio or, if the item is big enough, your local TV station. (For the TV station to be interested it would probably have to be on the scale of 'New contract saves 80 manufacturing jobs'.) Ensure you consider practicalities such as deadlines. If your local newspaper is weekly, being published on a Friday, it will probably have a cut off point during Wednesday when no further news (of this kind) will be accepted for that week.

Why not send out the press release to see what response you get? The very worst that can happen is you get ignored.

Demonstrating expertise

An important way of enhancing the reputation of your business is to demonstrate expertise. One very effective method is to write 'learned articles' for publication in the trade journals related to your sector, or perhaps the local (and occasionally national) press. Don't be put off by the term 'learned article'. I am not suggesting some weighty academic tome. Your article can be light and entertaining, yet still enhance your business's reputation. For example, if you run a pre-school nursery you could write an article entitled 'Top tips for keeping the terrible twos out of trouble'. The owner of a motor repair garage could produce an article on 'Five ways to keep your car trouble-free this winter'. The list of possibilities is endless, and whatever your business sector there are many suitable and interesting topics. Read through any business-related magazine and you will find examples of articles that will prompt ideas and inspire you.

What does this have to do with selling your business? A great deal. First, publicity increases awareness of your business. Secondly, handled well your reputation can be enhanced. And thirdly, it can lead directly to contacts and relationships that culminate in the sale of your business. I can vouch for the truth of this because it happened in my business. At the risk of being personal and boring, perhaps a brief case study might be useful in clarifying the key factors that worked for me.

Learned articles

My business partner and I ran a small but growing business offering outsourced procurement services to very large organizations (the specific details are not particularly important). As we won new contracts, we ensured that press releases were issued and became surprised at how easily we could attract positive attention in the trade press. They were hungry for interesting items to fill their pages.

Before setting up our enterprise, my background and that of my business partner had been as buyers for a very large supermarket group. We had spent hours sitting across the table from hundreds of sales people and had managed many tenders and awarded numerous major contracts. We realized that this experience was crucial to providing an effective service for our customers (and potential customers), as we were effectively tasked with buying better on their behalf than they could achieve themselves. This is how we earned our fees. I wrote a couple of articles entitled something like, 'Selling to big business; a buyer's perspective' and 'How to win a contract through tendering'. The articles were intended to be genuinely useful and interesting, but also to demonstrate a deep expertise within our business. The approach worked very successfully. Many magazines were interested in publishing the articles and I even got paid for them (a hugely pleasant surprise – imagine getting paid for self-publicity!). More to the point, feedback from suppliers, competitors and customers confirmed that the articles had been read and appreciated. It helped us move from being perceived as a 'start-up' business to a small but serious player in our sector. One competitor, with whom we were already on friendly terms, went on to buy our business. Was this just because of a couple of articles? Of course not, but the articles were important in consolidating our reputation.

What people think of your business is influenced by what they know about you. Ensure you communicate positive messages, and demonstrate your expertise. Do this often.

Sharing interesting data

Sharing interesting data is another way of demonstrating expertise. People love statistics – and they believe them. You may disagree with this statement, but please think again. Look at TV advertising. We all know how many cats prefer a certain type of tinned meat – correct: 8/10! Consider advertisements for beauty products – 82 per cent of women agreed that they look younger after using a certain cream. And it is not only advertising. I just picked up a trade-mortgage magazine that happened to be lying around in my office. Flicking through I found out that in February 2007 the average amount paid out in mortgage cash-backs in the UK dropped from £306 to £226. Why am I interested? I'm not in the least interested, but the magazine's regular readers must be – after all someone compiles and publishes the statistics each month. Statistics are impressive, and 92 per cent of people believe them (I just made that up).

One successful way to gather interesting and publishable information is to conduct a survey with a view to publishing interesting results. This might conjure up stressful images of people with clipboards chasing shoppers along the precinct, but this is only one possibility. For example, if you run a taxi service specializing in taking and collecting people from the airport, you could ask them to fill in a brief questionnaire during the journey. The list of possible questions is endless, so we will just consider a small number.

ABC Airport Taxis – Customer Questionnaire

Is your journey
Business   Pleasure
If you ticked pleasure, is your destination
Sun   Skiing   City   Other
How many times a year do you fly from x airport?
1   2   3   3+
What factors are most important when choosing an airport taxi service?
Reliability   Cost   Vehicle type   Vehicle cleanliness
24-hour service

Even these few simple questions could provide data to write numerous short yet interesting articles:

▌ 'Dog-town residents fly over twice a year on average'. A survey by ABC Airport taxis has revealed that 62 per cent of their customers from the Dog-town area fly at least twice a year, with 21 per cent flying on three or more occasions. According to Managing Director Mark Smith, this is up by a third on the results of last year. Mr Smith remarked... or,
▌ 'Vehicle cleanliness tops the poll for taxi firm users', or perhaps,
▌ 'Money-ville business users take to the sky'.

These are obviously slightly frivolous examples aimed at lightening a book examining a serious subject. But with a little effort, important data can be uncovered and used to improve the profile and reputation of your business.

Awards

Offering or sponsoring awards within your business sector can be an excellent way to raise your profile with key groups who may make up the most likely buyers of your business. I have worked with a number of businesses that use this method. One of them operates within the financial services sector and supports awards along the lines of 'West Yorkshire Independent Financial Adviser of the Year'. The other is a business providing creative marketing solutions and sponsors an award for visual artists. In both these cases funding the awards was not necessarily cheap, but the number of positive column inches provided by the press is phenomenal. It is an excellent way to create broad publicity in a narrow business sector.

Networking

Networking is a subject that takes me out of my comfort zone, and it may affect you similarly. The idea of standing in a group of strangers saying 'Hello I'm Andrew, what do you do?' fills me with dread. Two points to make here. First, if you don't like putting yourself in uncomfortable situations, *tough*. Selling a business for a very attractive price will require you to feel uncomfortable on occasions, so just get on with it. Secondly, networking has many forms – some of which are very pleasant. Here are a few ideas to get you thinking about networking opportunities.

Start with the people you know

Everybody knows people who know people. If you were to write down all of your business contacts, plus all of your personal contacts, you would end up with a reasonably long list. Popular and gregarious people might have a list extending to a hundred or so, and miserable plods like me might think of, say, 40 names. Assuming they all know at least 40 people, we can conclude that the people *we* know, know 1,600 people between them. Not a bad network. If you wanted to you could ring up any of these people and say 'Julie McMillan is a friend of mine. I hope you don't mind me calling but she suggested you may be a good person to talk to about...'. Chances are they would listen, and may even be able to help or at least be willing to discuss your topic. Obviously you need to let friend Julie know what you are up to, just in case she takes exception and your personal network of 40 becomes 39. An even better approach would be to get Julie to effect a brief introduction – perhaps by a short e-mail. Some of my best business contacts have come from people I know who know people, and I have always been happy to return favours. Whenever I get the chance to introduce business contacts who could be helpful to one another I do so – and it has never backfired or caused trouble.

Use formal networking groups

Your local Chamber of Commerce will organize events in your region specifically created to allow you to network. You may feel a bit of a prat, but then so does everyone else – and I can confirm from experience that you won't just meet useful contacts but also interesting and nice people. Don't attend these groups with the mindset of a prowler, more someone looking for interesting discussions. A big tip when networking is to show more interest in *them* than yourself. By getting people to talk about themselves you can find out all kinds of interesting and useful information, and they will like you for showing interest. (A good tip that someone gave me is, 'Get to formal networking events early.' The logic is, if you are first in the room people will have to approach you. If you arrive late everyone will be chatting and you will struggle to break into the mini-groups that have formed – at least without being pushy!)

Network gently and regularly

A contact of mine is an excellent networker. He takes time each day to drop brief e-mails, pass on a little news or to ask 'How are things?' Using this method he keeps his network alive without being at all pushy or asking for things. Think about this. How many times have you lost contact with a business acquaintance or ex-colleague? You don't speak for years and then they call you out of the blue. When this happens you can usually predict that, a) they have lost their job, or b) they are getting divorced and are using their (by now extinct) network to shore themselves up. Wouldn't it have been better if they had found time to stay in touch during the intervening period? Wouldn't you feel more motivated to help them/meet them/support them if they hadn't just called when they needed something? Stay in touch with people even when you don't need anything.

Help others

If you can make a phone call or provide another small service for people on the periphery of your network, do so. You will find yourself paid back in kind several times over. It is better to give than to receive, and it costs about the same in the long run.

What would you like people to say?

So far in this chapter we have covered *who* you might wish to communicate with and *how* you will be successful in doing so without a large marketing or PR budget. Another important consideration involves asking 'What would I like my customers/suppliers/competitors/whoever to say about my business?' Obviously the range of answers is infinite, but it is worth taking time to prioritize what factors would most impact a potential buyer's interest level, and influence their approach to valuation.

Activity: How do you wish to be perceived?

Consider the following list. Rank them in order of importance from a potential buyer's perspective (1 = most important):

Excellent service – doesn't let customers down.
High on value (low prices).
Reputation for quality.
Consistently growing.
Large geographical coverage.
Friendly service.
High quality – high prices.
Fast delivery.
Innovative designs.
Leading edge.
Extended opening hours (high availability).
Broad range of options.

You probably found the above activity quite difficult. Perhaps you want to have a reputation for all of the listed attributes. Some will have more appeal to prospective buyers that others – but what these factors are will vary depending upon your sector and circumstances.

Formal marketing activities

Although this chapter has focused heavily on the DIY aspect of marketing, you should not assume that involving professionals to help would be a bad move. Specialist marketing companies do tend to be quite expensive – especially from the perspective of smaller customers – but there may be a solid business case for employing the services of a marketing professional. Perhaps you don't have the time to invest in a regular and consistent PR programme. Maybe you honestly feel you don't have the necessary skills within your business. My simple advice is 'Make sure you find a way to get back more cash from your marketing efforts than you spend on them.' When you think about it, it's not a bad definition for effective marketing. Unfortunately, you will find it difficult to get guarantees from marketers, and you should remember that 'half of all marketing activity is wasted, but we don't know which half'.

Quality materials

One small matter that can significantly affect the perception people have of your business is the quality of marketing materials. Too many successful small businesses sell themselves short by having cheap, naff stationery and poor marketing materials. It is increasingly necessary for businesses to have a website – not specifically to sell through, but just as a kind of electronic brochure. If you randomly search websites belonging to small businesses on the internet you will find that quality varies markedly. If your website has been constructed with little thought or investment, that is exactly how people will perceive your business. I am not suggesting it is appropriate to find an expensive web designer, or that your website should have the functionality of Amazon.co.uk, merely that you ensure the quality of the materials you present to the outside world matches the quality of service (or products) that your business aspires to. Someone once advised me that 'The only thing worse than being broke, is looking broke.' Your website, brochures and stationery can create an image of being broke, or of success. Think clearly about the image that you wish to convey.

FINDING THE BUYER

Marketing activities such as those described above can be as broad or as narrow in focus as you choose to make them. You can focus on a geographical area, or a specific sector. You may even focus on becoming noticed by just a few competitors. I guess there are really two key stages to these activities. The first is to get noticed and broaden your reputation. The second involves directly finding a buyer. In doing so you may employ the services of a business broker, rely on the network of your other professional advisers, or simply do it yourself. Having had a reputation-building marketing plan in place for a couple of years will make the DIY approach easier, and it is certainly possible to find a buyer directly yourself.

The serial entrepreneur sells again

In Chapter 1 I described how Tony Gill found a buyer for his first business. You may recall that this involved little more than conducting research on competitors (to identify which companies where large enough – and acquisitive enough), and then picking up the telephone. An effective and successful approach. However, in marketing and selling his second business Tony needed to develop a longer-term exit plan, and had to ensure his business was in good shape ahead of discussions with potential buyers.

Tony's second business was in the same sector as his previous enterprise. This time around he had significant resources and could afford to invest large sums in equipment that should ensure production was efficient enough to make the business competitive. The business was successful and expanded rapidly. However, the market had shifted. While a number of competitors existed within the United Kingdom, there were also many new entrants into the market from other European countries, and especially from Eastern Europe. These competitors had significantly lower wage costs than any business producing in the United Kingdom, and the resulting over-capacity caused chaos in the UK market.

What would be an appropriate response to this situation? Tony focused on two distinct activities. First, he took time to get to know his European competitors. He contacted them, met them, and in small ways worked on projects with them. Through this approach trust and understanding developed. Part of the strategy was to create interest in buying Tony's UK operations in the minds of the European competitors. The second aspect of his strategy was to consider a takeover or merger with another UK competitor, with a view to increasing market share and gaining production efficiencies that would enable the merged business to compete more effectively. He quickly found a match in a similar sized competitor that was, in his words, 'very good at production, but pretty crap at marketing and selling'. The competitor was making very modest profits, and was certainly struggling to remain successful within the increasingly challenging market. The competitor firm had two directors, one of whom was interested in retirement. Tony bought his shares, and gradually merged the two businesses to a position where all production was on one site, and sales and marketing activities were combined under one company name.

The result of this activity was that a number of European competitors became very interested in the enlarged UK operation and a firm offer was received for the business. The offer was financially lucrative but came with a difficult clause attached: the prospective purchasers wanted to lock Tony into the business for five years after the sale was completed. Part of the value they saw was in his skills. How did Tony handle the situation? We pick up the story in Chapter 9 – surviving a lock-in period.

Even if, like our serial entrepreneur, you decide to adopt a very direct approach to selling, it will be useful to have 'warmed up' the marketplace with effective reputation-building PR. For many people, finding the buyer will involve detailed consideration of the market, their businesses role within it, competitors, and why someone would be interested in buying. What message would you give to potential buyers? What will be your story? Creating a sale memorandum can provide a useful and disciplined approach.

THE SALE MEMORANDUM

One aspect of marketing your business is the preparation of the sale memorandum. This is a document that sets out key information about your business and the marketplace it operates in. The document is specifically intended to be of interest to potential buyers or investors. Achieving this requires creating a compelling story, and supporting it with clear figures.

Many firms employ an accountant or business broker to create the document. There are two reasons why this might be an effective approach. First, they have significant experience in doing so and will hopefully have developed a format that has historically proved to be successful. Secondly, they can create and issue the document confidentially, without the name of your business being mentioned. This may be a vitally important factor as many business owners do not want employees or customers to be aware that a sale is being considered. A challenging situation; you need prospective purchasers to be aware that you wish to sell but dare not tell anyone! If you are considering paying someone to prepare the document on your behalf it would be a good idea to ask to see a couple of examples of documents that they have previously prepared. In reviewing these you might find that you could do a better job yourself (or at least pinch a few of their ideas).

The following section provides ideas on how a sales memorandum might be structured.

Structure of the sale memorandum

The content of the sale memorandum will depend on your specific business. It will also be affected by how tightly you wish to protect your anonymity in the early stages of searching for a buyer. If you prepare and issue the document yourself it will be more difficult to remain anonymous. Think about this factor carefully.

There are nine key headings that will be useful in preparing the sale memorandum:

1. Market description.
2. Why your business is successful in this market.
3. People.
4. Technology.
5. Property.
6. Financials.
7. Price and brief commercial considerations.
8. Testimonials or references.
9. Disclaimer and confidentiality.

Each of the above headings is worth considering in turn.

1. Market description

What is the size of your market (consider whether your service is the local, national or international market)? What are the trends within the market? Is it growing, declining or static? Who are the key competitors in the market? What is their market share? How do you compete in the market? For example, do you offer budget-priced products or aim to maintain a high price point (are you EasyJet or British Airways)? Who are key suppliers in your marketplace? Describe where you sit within the supply chain. The more specific you can be on all of these aspects the better. If you can't accurately list and describe your key competitors it will be difficult for anyone outside your business sector to understand your role within it.

2. Why your business is successful in this market

How does your business compete? Why does your business make money? How will it continue to make money in the longer term? What is unique or different about your products, services or brand? How does your product portfolio sit in the market?

Any potential buyer will be looking for answers to these questions, so help them by providing the answers.

If you business relies on long-term contracts and has been successful in securing a number of them, say so. You don't have to name customer names at this stage, but if (for example) two-thirds of projected income over the next three years is already contracted you should make it clear in the document.

3. People

This is an interesting topic. Does your business rely on you to function properly on a daily basis? Is a team in place to ensure it functions properly when you are not there? Assuming you wish to avoid a protracted 'lock-in' situation, having a positive answer to these questions is crucial. Within the people section you should fully describe the responsibilities, skills and abilities of your executive team. Consider including brief CVs of key staff. Also describe the broader workforce. Explain how you attract and retain the best staff. Comment on your staff turnover levels. If relevant, describe the availability of appropriately qualified staff in your sector or region.

4. Technology

Does your business rely on advanced technology? Have you invested in state-of-the-art equipment? Even very modest businesses these days invest significantly in IT equipment. Ensure you describe how systems and processes support your business activities.

5. Property

Property and location are important for most businesses, and are absolutely vital for some. Ensure you clearly describe whether property is freehold or leasehold, and comment on arrangements after the sale. Perhaps you hold the freehold on the property but wish to offer an attractive lease to the new owner. Ensure you make the situation absolutely clear in the document.

6. Financials

Perhaps this is the trickiest aspect of the sale memorandum. Supply too much information at this stage and you risk giving away commercially sensitive information. Provide too little and people have no real idea of what is on offer. Perhaps at this stage it is best to offer only headline information. At a later stage, when you have had a better chance to assess interest levels and how genuine your prospective buyers are, you can offer full financial disclosure under the cover of a detailed confidentiality agreement.

If you are happy to disclose significant financial details at this stage, the key numbers should include:

- Historical figures over at least three years.
- Information from profit and loss accounts and balance sheets.
- Cash flow information.
- Revenue and cost projections for future years.
- Stock holding.
- Key costs of the business.

7. Price and brief commercial considerations

How much are you asking for the business? Putting a price on the table is tricky. Ask for too little and you give 'free' value to the buyer. Ask for too much and there may be no buyer. If you have considered the performance and future prospects of your business carefully, have utilized a number of valuation techniques and have thoroughly sense-checked your numbers with a qualified adviser, you should have some comfort that the sum being requested is reasonable, and can be justified by the supporting data. Sometimes you just have to be brave. However strong your analysis, the final decision on the asking price rests with you.

8. Testimonials or references

Having someone else validate the claims made within the sale memorandum is important. This may be a customer who is prepared to confirm in writing what a valued supplier you are. It could be your bank manager or accountant who is prepared to confirm that the key figures quoted are correct. Having the views of others to support your story can only be positive.

9. Disclaimer and confidentiality

You may wish to take legal advice on this aspect. At the very least include a disclaimer within your document to the effect that all information is provided in good faith but is subject to the buyer satisfying themselves of the total accuracy of all data provided. In addition, it is a good idea to have a brief confidentiality agreement drawn up that can be signed by the prospective buyer ahead of receiving a copy of the sale memorandum. See Chapter 7 for further information on confidentiality agreements.

Chapter summary

▮ Public relations is the art of building and managing a positive reputation. People won't buy your business if they don't know it exists.

▮ It is possible to achieve effective PR with a little thought, careful planning and a very modest budget.

▮ There are many reasons for communicating with people on behalf of your business – for example a new contract, new premises or even a new idea.

▮ Think about *what* you wish to communicate to *whom* and *how. When* can also be important – news is usually, well, *new*.

▮ Writing articles, creating questionnaires and sponsoring prizes are effective methods of generating interest – and information.

▮ Never underestimate the power of networking. Effective networking does not have to be formal or smarmy – it can be good fun.

▮ Good PR will help you to find a buyer when the time comes to do so. At this stage, directly approaching potential buyers is proven to be successful.

▮ Even if you plan to directly approach a predetermined list of prospective buyers, softening up the market with effective PR can only be helpful.

6

Managing the Sale Process

The first piece of advice in this chapter is that you take note of the chapter title: *Managing the sale process*. While you will almost certainly rely on your professional advisers to handle many aspects of the sale, you should recognize that overall responsibility rests with you. Obviously you have been running a business for some time and are therefore fully used to taking the lead, but as we mentioned in Chapter 4 on professional advisers, many people seem to leave their own thoughts behind when crossing the threshold of their accountant or lawyer. You must remain in charge. However skilled and motivated your advisers may be, it is you who has the most to gain – or lose – at the end of the process.

Obviously the sale process will vary depending on your specific circumstances. However, having spoken to a number of commercial lawyers and accountants in preparing this book, it is clear that key elements of the process are relevant to almost all business sales. Finding a buyer was covered in detail in Chapter 1, so the starting point for this chapter is that a potential buyer is in place. At this juncture an important question arises: do you involve your lawyer or accountant (or both) in early stage discussions with the potential buyer? It may be useful to relate a real-world example in considering the answer. How did our serial entrepreneur approach the early discussions with his buyer?

The serial entrepreneur

As we saw in Chapter 1, our serial entrepreneur resolved the question of who would buy his business by directly ringing up a larger competitor. His approach was simple, direct and effective. The competitor was interested and the very next day the managing director arrived to begin discussions.

During discussions a number of crucial decisions were taken that would affect the sale process, and the financial outcome. One decision was agreeing the price to be paid. The seller had decided that he would take the average of the last three years' net profits and apply a multiple of six (see Chapter 2 for an explanation of the 'multiple' method of valuation). Was this the 'correct' price? If you have read Chapter 2 you will know the answer is that we will never know, because there is no fixed method of valuing a business. However, if you were selling a business for a very large sum, wouldn't you consider it sensible to ask an experienced accountant whether the price agreed is realistic? You could ask whether the multiple agreed is similar to that applied to other recent sales of similar businesses. It may also be sensible to consider whether assets have been realistically accounted for. And what about cash? Is the cash currently held by the business included in the sale? All of these questions, and more, would benefit from the attention of an accountant with recent experience in business disposals, but in this case advice was not requested. I can't help thinking that this was a serious omission, and our serial entrepreneur now agrees. (Having said that, he is the one with all the money in the bank, so he doesn't appear to be too upset.)

The process for conducting 'due diligence' was also agreed during early discussions. Due diligence is the process by which the buyer checks out the business to ensure that the sale price agreed is sensible, and that there are no skeletons in the cupboard that will emerge after the sale has been concluded. The due diligence process will be covered in detail in the next chapter. If you are not familiar with the process, in simple terms it is analogous to the steps taken when buying a house. You ask a surveyor to put an independent value on the house, and check out the structure to make sure it isn't falling down and that woodworm has not infested the joists. Your solicitor also ensures that the house is actually the property of the people purporting to sell it, and that there are no unpleasant surprises that may occur, such as the appearance of a dual-carriageway where the rose beds currently lie. As you will understand after reading the next chapter, the process for 'checking out' potential problems in a house sale is nothing like as complicated or extensive as those that occur during the sale of a business.

In the case of our entrepreneur, he agreed to let people representing the prospective purchaser into the business, to check things out for themselves. They stayed for nine months and had access to all financial, customer and supplier information. It probably occurs to you that this was not a good idea, to say the least. A big part of the value of any business lies in its data and processes. If your competitors were to find out this information they could probably damage your business very badly, and very quickly. I asked an experienced commercial lawyer for his thoughts, but he just rolled his eyes heavenwards and made a strange whistling noise. But Tony was trusting, and as it happens his trust was not misplaced as the sale was eventually successfully concluded. Having said that, the original sale price was reduced as a result of the due diligence process. Could this have been avoided if professional advisers had been involved earlier? Who knows, but for the sums involved it is not worth taking a risk.

Of course, one of the great things about being in business is the opportunity to learn as you go. Next time around, Tony managed the sale process very differently.

We have now uncovered two pieces of advice. First, take control of the process yourself, and second, involve advisers early. The worst that can happen is that you lose a little money on their fees should the sale falter. It is small consolation, but at least they are tax deductible.

HEADS OF TERMS

All of the accountants and solicitors that I spoke to in researching the book recommended the creation of a 'heads of terms' document. This sets out the principles surrounding the deal, without necessarily getting into fine contractual detail. I guess there are many benefits to doing this, but two seem most obvious. First, it allows all parties to quickly understand what everyone is agreeing to, and second, it can be used as a kind of 'referee document' when arguments arise later. If it is not in the heads of terms it was not part of what was originally agreed. One lawyer summarized the benefit of the document by noting that 'it saves time, confusion and cost'.

You may not be surprised to learn that the accountants I spoke to felt that they could successfully draw up heads of terms on behalf of the client, but the lawyers believed that only they could create a robust and effective document. Having been through a business sale process myself, I believe a lawyer is best placed to draft the document, as many of the terms are of a legal rather than financial nature. Of course there is nothing to stop your accountant having a look at the draft document to see if anything requires adding or amending. The content of the heads of term document will be covered in detail in Chapter 7.

PREFERRED BIDDER

Unless your business is very small, and the sale relatively simple, both parties will incur significant costs as the process proceeds. The buyer may well request that the heads of terms acknowledges their 'exclusive rights' to pursue the deal. This is sometimes referred to as appointing the supplier as 'preferred bidder'. Basically the buyer will want written assurance that you will not enter into discussions with any other potential buyer unless and until the sale process between you and them fails and termination of the process is agreed. In other words, if you secretly enter discussions with other potential buyers that result in the sale being completed with them, the preferred buyer could potentially sue you for damages, and to recover costs incurred by them.

BE ORGANIZED

Once the sale process begins you will be staggered at the range and volume of information that is requested and provided. You may anticipate that the process will be similar to an annual audit, but you will be wrong. An enormous mountain of information will be generated and if you have not kept your administration in order, you are going to find yourself sinking under the weight of requests for documentation. The best advice is not just that you are organized, but that you become so well ahead of beginning the sale process. Here is just some of the information that you will need to have to hand, which must be accurate and up to date, if you are to avoid problems further down the track:

▌ All of the statutory books of the company up to date (for example, the register of shareholders, board minutes and memorandum of association).
▌ Registration documents.
▌ Insurance documents.
▌ Accounts going back several years.
▌ Tax records, returns and computations.
▌ VAT records, returns and computations.
▌ Details of any leases or hire purchase agreements.
▌ Details of any mortgages or other agreements.
▌ Details of financial arrangements (any lending or borrowing of any kind).
▌ Accurate and up-to-date management accounts for the current year.
▌ Details of credit terms offered to customers.
▌ Details of any joint ventures or partnerships.
▌ Details of any pending commercial disputes.
▌ Any claims pending by suppliers or customers.
▌ Full details on all employees, including contracts of employment, full history, full personal details and information on any claims or disputes arising from employees.
▌ Asset register of all owned assets.
▌ All contracts with suppliers, customers or others.
▌ Details of any product or service guarantees.

THE LAWYER AS PROJECT MANAGER

Although it is your overall responsibility to manage the process, a good solicitor will act as project manager for the legal aspects of the sale process. In doing so he or she will interpret and screen all requests for information from other parties, and ensure that the flow of data is sensibly managed. If you have chosen a legal firm that offers a broad range of services, your lawyer will be able to draw on the experience of other specialists within the firm. This may include, for example, a property lawyer or employment specialist. Hopefully you will have chosen a commercial lawyer who handles many business transactions each year, who will be able to advise and reassure throughout the process. In doing so he or she will not just identify the things that are important, but also the things that are not so important. There are only so many things you can worry about at any given time.

TAX CLEARANCE

Having agreed a sale price and payment schedule, your accountant will be in a position to advise on matters relating to taxation. *Always take tax advice.* The sale of your business will almost certainly involve paying tax on capital gains, and could also attract income tax and other forms of taxation. It may also be sensible to discuss longer-term issues with both your lawyer and accountant, as inheritance tax currently stands at 40 per cent in the United Kingdom, and you may find the threshold for paying the tax surprisingly low.

One way to avoid nasty tax surprises in the future (apart from ensuring you speak to an accountant) is to apply to the tax authorities for clearance. Basically this involves your accountant writing to HM Revenue and Customs with details of the deal you have agreed and how he or she believes taxation would apply. HMRC either 'approves' the approach by agreeing (in principle) with the stated tax position, or advises how it considers the deal would be taxed.

OTHER PARTIES

Many deals will involve a third-party lender who will provide the finance (and for larger deals there may be several lenders). This will obviously be the case when the sale is in the form of a management buyout (MBO). Having another party involved means (yes you guessed it) another firm of lawyers, and another series of requests for information. Generally the lender's lawyers will not become involved in any detail until the latter stages of the deal are being completed, but of course they will want to scrutinize all aspects of the agreement. As it is the lender's money that will make the deal possible, you will want to offer every assistance in approving release of the funds. The problem is of course that part of the collateral to guarantee the loan will be the assets of your business, so the lender will take just as much care – and cover just as much due diligence – as your buyer.

NEGOTIATION SKILLS

I have spent a fair proportion of my working life buying and selling, and have trained hundreds of people in the art of negotiation. Nevertheless, selling your business is probably a once in a lifetime opportunity, so

I am nervous about regaling you with my usual bullish approach to maximizing the result in negotiation situations. Treat this as a serious 'health warning': negotiating effectively involves risk, and generally speaking the harder you push, the greater the risk of an overall failure to agree a deal. Having said that, you did not become a successful business person by being weak and nervous. Only you know your circumstances, so reflect on the following suggestions, but determine your approach wisely.

If you want it badly, you get it badly

If you are desperate to sell quickly, and only have one potential buyer, your negotiating position is weakened. That's obvious. But what is less obvious is that the more you convey the desperation, the more the buyer will push downwards on price, or other aspects of the deal. A successful businessman once advised, 'There is only one thing worse than being broke, and that's looking broke.' By logical extension, there is only one thing worse than being desperate and that is appearing to be so. Keep an outwardly positive demeanour at all times.

It's about them

Having spent considerable time talking to your accountant, lawyer, bank manager and anyone else who has an intelligent opinion, you have calculated what you consider to be a fair and sensible price for your business. But wait: does this mean you have to show your hand and put a price firmly on the table? Perhaps you will have to, but what about an approach that says to the potential buyer 'Let's look at the key aspects of the business together and agree a sensible price.' You never know, they might offer more than you anticipated.

On a broader point, the purpose of a negotiation is to find out how far the other party is prepared to go and gently take them there. This involves focusing most of your attention on them. This approach has two benefits. First, it stops you thinking about your own desperation to sell. Second, it means you uncover information that may be helpful in progressing the sale. Put another way, asking questions is always preferable to answering them. Think about discussions undertaken with your lawyer. She asks questions and you answer them. When she has enough information to advise what course of action to take, she uses the information gained to support her argument. She appears to be clever because she is. Not because she is a qualified solicitor, but as a result of asking questions and knowing how to use the information gained to solve the problem.

In negotiations it is generally risky to be talking for too much of the time. A skilled negotiator will use what he or she hears against you. Luckily, skilled negotiators are quite rare.

Think in threes

My experience in literally hundreds of negotiations (I was a buyer with a large retailer for many years) is that people always seem to jump about in very large round numbers. For example, if you are asking £300,000 for your business, the chances are the buyer will make an offer along the lines of £270,000. Not only is the £30,000 'discount' a nice round figure, but it also represents 10 per cent of the asking price. Using round figures is so commonplace that I almost consider it a 'law of human nature'. I am not a psychologist, but this tendency really does seem to be hard-wired into our brains – at least in Western European nations. Not only does the buyer act in this way, but you do too. The chances are in this scenario that many of you would either come back with a figure of, say, £290,000 or £280,000, and may even suggest 'splitting the difference' at £285,000. You too are caught in the game of jumping around in large numbers. If you had, for example, counter-offered £280,000 you have given away 20 grand in one sentence. Twenty thousand pounds is a lot of money – enough to buy two or three small cars or many luxury holidays abroad, and you just gave it away in a single breath. Why not come back with a response along the lines of: 'Thanks for your offer. I really can't even consider the price you suggested. Let me tell you what I can do. If you agree to make payment in full on contractual completion, I will agree to reduce the price to £297,000. Do we have a deal?'

Notice the words used in the last paragraph. 'Let me tell you what I can do.' In negotiations too much time is spent telling the other party what you can't do. The words 'If you… then I' are also crucial. This involves you making a concession subject to getting something back. It is a conditional offer. If the other party doesn't agree, it can be removed from the table without fuss – this stops the other party banking all of your concessions without giving any back. If you start out with a sensible figure, and make your concessions relatively small and subject to getting things back in return, you will conclude a good deal. Remember, negotiations are not just about price. Pre-prepare a list of things that you can ask for, or trade in return for concessions. Examples may include:

- Payment terms (more cash on completion).
- Limiting warranties (perhaps to a one-year rather than two-year period).

▌ Time spent locked into the business after the sale.
▌ An offer to stay in the business for a short while to conclude an effective handover ('If you agree to my price of £297,000 I will work in the business for a month and set up meetings for you with all key customers.')

There are always many things that can be traded in this way.

The opening offer is crucial

I have evidence that demonstrates how crucial the starting point is from the seller's point of view. But we shouldn't need evidence – it is obvious. The starting point is the most you will achieve, and depending on the other party (and other factors) you may well be forced to accept a much lower figure. The solution is obvious – but also dangerous. Open with a high price to give yourself the best chance of maximizing the final deal. Of course, if you open too high there may be no negotiation at all. This is a very difficult judgement call.

Feeling uncomfortable is normal

Even experienced business people find the process of negotiation uncomfortable. I can think of three reasons why this may be the case. First, negotiation is simply difficult. It involves making the other party submit to your position, even when their desired outcome is quite different. Realize that influencing other people is difficult. Second, fear of failure is ever present. The negotiation in front of you might be the biggest and most important deal of your life. Worrying about a successful outcome might be counterproductive, but it is understandable. Third, selfishly pursuing your own interests might not come naturally – our parents bring us up to be considerate and tolerant, but successful negotiation involves suppressing these instincts to some extent.

How can this discomfort be overcome? Well, just recognizing that this is normal might help a little. Further, although the best 'inner' attitude in a negotiation is based on being selfish and determined, outwardly the most appropriate approach is one of jointly looking to find an amicable solution. Inwardly you might be thinking 'There is no way I will drop my price to that level,' while you say 'Thank you for that suggestion. Unfortunately that kind of figure doesn't work for me and I can't consider it further. However, let me tell you what I can do... .' If you say polite and sensible things you will feel sensible and polite.

Remember, in a negotiation situation you are effectively being paid to feel uncomfortable.

Should you involve a solicitor?

So far in this section we have approached negotiation as if it were a single event. Of course it may well be much more protracted than that – and probably will be. For example, you might have an initial negotiation where the 'deal' is agreed in outline. Aspects such as price, payment schedule and timescales will probably be established. Should you have your solicitor present at this time, or perhaps your accountant? It is not really necessary to do so, but if you feel that the support would help, why not? All you have to lose are fees for the time expended. Later in the process, however, you may be negotiating equally important aspects that do require specialist legal input. One big area to be negotiated involves warranties and indemnities, which are basically things the seller agrees to protect the buyer against. A good solicitor will attempt to limit your exposure as much as possible, and will be much better at identifying implications that you perhaps haven't considered. Always involve your solicitor in this type of negotiation.

One benefit of using your solicitor in negotiations is that you can blame him or her for being overly aggressive, while in reality fully supporting his or her position. It is probably less dangerous for your solicitor to upset or annoy your potential buyer than doing so yourself. Ideally, of course, neither of you will upset anyone because – externally at least – you will be approaching the deal in a fair, open and reasonable manner.

Leave your ego at home

In my experience 'ego' is the biggest stumbling block in concluding an effective negotiation. Outwardly wanting to win, and above all wanting to appear to have won at the expense of others, is really very unhelpful. For me negotiation is about getting the money (or the lifting of an indemnity or whatever). If the other party feels that you have 'won', by definition they will consider themselves losers, which does not do anyone any good – especially during the further negotiations that lie ahead. Choose you words carefully. Consider using phrases such as:

'I really am trying to find ways to help but we just can't agree to that clause.'
'Is there another way to look at this that would be acceptable to all parties?'

'Unfortunately we have reached our minimum position on this point. Can we accept this in its current form and look to help in other ways?'

Phrases such as these are designed to make the other party feel you are looking for solutions rather than making demands.

Beware formulas

One of the most common methods of agreeing the sale price is the multiple method described in Chapter 2. You may, for example, have proposed that the sale price will be seven times the average post-tax profit over the last three years. If the profit figure is £120,000, the sale price proposed will obviously extend to £840,000. What if your potential buyer challenges the seven-times multiple and offers 6.7 times instead? Doesn't sound a big deal does it? Well, if you agree to this concession you have just said goodbye to £36,000. Does this sound obvious? I have been involved in many negotiations when formulas were being used and both parties appear to have become detached from the cash sums involved. Always convert formulas to cash before reaching agreement.

Exploit the final momentum

Negotiations tend to go through three phases. The first involves everyone chatting amicably whilst drinking coffee, and studiously avoiding anything that might resemble a negotiation. After a while the business begins to get serious and we enter the phase that is both uncomfortable and stressful. It's probably best to call this the, erm, negotiation. Finally, there is the bit at the end where hands are shaken and we all get back to being friendly. Does this sound familiar? The most dangerous part of the negotiation is near the end when you are close to agreement, and perhaps have settled all of the main points. It is in this situation when you are all feeling more relaxed (and keen to get to the final phase) that you are most likely to make concessions. Remember, you will have a long time afterwards to regret rash decisions. Do not relax until all key points are finalized. Where possible, ask for a bit more at the end. They will probably happily concede.

Negotiation summary

Plan your negotiations well. Take time to consider all aspects of the process from the other party's point of view. Remember effective negotiation focuses on 'them, not you'. You need to invest time to think through what the other party might want: how they might act and react. Put yourself in their position and bounce around a whole range of scenarios. Be prepared and have a list of possible things to trade. Know what you can do and what you can't do. You will be perceived as much more positive if you remain focused on what you *can do*.

Conducting an effective negotiation is difficult for many reasons. If you find the whole process uncomfortable, you are in good company – almost everyone struggles to be effective in negotiations – and this probably includes your opponent. If you leave the negotiation feeling slightly bruised and unhappy, you have probably done a good job. If you depart feeling the negotiation was a breeze, and light-heartedly skip out of the building, you can be fairly sure that money was left on the table.

MANAGING TIMESCALES

Selling a business is quite a complex process, and is not necessarily a quick one. How quickly you can move from initial discussions to completion many depend on many factors, for example:

- how large and complex the deal is;
- how many locations are involved;
- how challenging the due diligence process will be;
- availability and access to information;
- whether there is an international dimension;
- how many parties are involved (lending organizations for example);
- the level of urgency – either party might have a need to either accelerate the process or slow it down (for example to allow time to raise cash);
- production of year-end audit/accounts.

All of these factors, and many others, may limit the pace at which the deal can be progressed. However, many factors are possible to control and if both parties have a shortened timescale in mind it should be achievable (with a little goodwill from your professional advisers) to make quicker progress. How long might the process take? A modest sized deal could be completed in around two to three months. A large and complex deal might take two or three times as long.

One of the key issues involved in managing timescales relates to effective 'communication'. Part of me always feels that communication is one of those woolly, touchy-feely topics beloved by people with business cards confirming their status as a 'strategy consultant' or other nefarious creature. However, in the context of selling a business, effective communication is essential if you are to ensure the process is controlled and stays on track. The section below considers the issue of communication in some detail.

COMMUNICATION

How do you know what your lawyer is doing on your behalf? Is the buyer still happy with the deal agreed? Are employees wondering about the intentions of the people in suits who are crawling all over the business? (In the absence of information they will pick a worst case scenario and believe that.) All of these are issues involve communication. It will pay to put time and resources into the task of getting the right message to each party as quickly, regularly and effectively as possible. Before considering communication as a specific business-sale issue, it may be useful to reflect on broader themes.

Rules of effective communication

The aren't really too many firm rules on the concept of effective communication. After all, people are not all the same and there is no single 'right way' to communicate. However, some approaches certainly work better than others. For example, we could state a rule to the effect that 'the recipients need to believe what they hear'. Too obvious? Well, there have been many times in my professional life when people (for example my employer) have formally told me something that I didn't believe, and I suspect the same is true for you. If the recipients do not believe what you tell them, not only have you failed to effectively get the message across, but damage has probably been done in the process. By the way, this is not the same as saying you are lying, just that the other person does not believe you.

Think about the whole concept of 'spin' that surrounded the United Kingdom's New Labour government in the late 1990s. So much effort was put into crafting and controlling communications that people began to disbelieve information almost on principle. This leads us onto another issue that compounds the problem. The result of communication is what the recipient hears, not what you think you said. People generally hear what they expect to hear, which can be a major blockage to getting your message across. One of the big problems in communication lies in the fact that we are 'telling' rather than 'asking'. If you tell people things and don't include a feedback mechanism, there is no opportunity to test whether what you meant to say was really heard. Take a very simple (and very fictitious) example.

What was said...

'I am pleased to announce that with immediate effect, Smoggins Engineering Ltd is owned by Smelterside Wire Group. I am sure that this new venture will deliver a successful and profitable future for all employees within the group, and both businesses can look forward to an exciting and challenging future. Thank you'. (Thinks... I am now on my way to cash this rather large cheque.)

What was heard...

'We've been sold down the river. Smelterside only wants the customer contracts. It will close down this factory and move the equipment it needs to its own works. I better start looking for another job.'

Which perspective is true? Maybe neither. Perhaps Smelterside has no intention of closing down Smoggins' factory. The problem is that people make announcements and then believe they have effectively communicated. The outgoing chairman probably believes – really believes – that he has reassured the workforce. He would probably be appalled to hear what is going on in the mind of the recipients of his message. This gives us a clue to an effective approach. If you need to make an effective communication on issues that matter (especially where you need people to do something or act differently) you have to go out of your way to generate feedback. This is the only way to find out what was heard, what people think, and what they are planning to do. This is why, in broad terms, asking is better than telling. So, in the case of Smoggins, the chairman would have done much better to agree a detailed communication programme (with the directors of Smelterside) that positively sought out feedback that could be addressed. The board should obviously have been able to predict the negative response from some members of staff and should have developed a strategy for dealing with it. The strategy must include feedback, or some other aspect of 'asking' rather than 'telling'. Anytime you 'tell' people anything, you have to make assumptions about how they will receive the information. When important commercial issues are at stake, should the opportunity be taken to test those assumptions? If you believe my example to be slightly unreal and ridiculous, I disagree. I have worked in organizations that communicated big announcements in exactly the way that the Smoggins' chairman does. In fact, I can even admit to doing it myself.

Writing, e-mail or spoken word?

Which is the best form of communication? Clearly it depends on the importance of the message – or more accurately the importance of the outcome of the message. My favourite example of how not to do it involves the workers of Accident Group, who were made redundant by text message. I am a big fan of the text message, and my daughters regularly send a text along the lines of 'wen yur pikin me up?', but I am less confident about its role in laying-off workers. Accident Group is not the only example of this phenomenon. A shop worker was recently sacked by text and her unrepentant boss was quoted as saying that the approach was appropriate, as texting is 'part of youth culture'. I can't help feeling that sacking by text will never be appropriate, but age may play a part in my thinking.

As a general rule, common sense will prevail. If you are negotiating the key points of the sale agreement, clearly a face-to-face meeting would be best. However, if your business is in Scunthorpe but the buyer is located in Seattle, many important discussions may need to take place by telephone or e-mail. Practicalities are important, but you should also consider that experts warn us of the importance of non-verbal communication. I read recently that in a face-to-face meeting less than 10 per cent of communication occurs via the words. The rest is accounted for by body posture, gestures, voice inflection and so on. While I wonder how the experts can empirically know the percentages, I don't doubt the overall accuracy of their conclusions. And I guess that e-mails are even worse. Cold words on an electronic page can appear much colder and more brutal than the writer intended. If I were to e-mail you that 'your suggestion is unacceptable', it would be easy to for you to feel affronted. However, if I called you it would be much easier to soften the impact. Think carefully about the appropriate means of communication. Don't necessarily do what is easiest. Take the option that will be most effective.

Pre-completion communication

For all but the simplest business sale there will probably be at least half a dozen parties involved in the process, including the buyer and seller, plus lawyers and accountants representing each side. At the outset of the process you should agree the formal lines of communication. For example, lawyers will probably deal directly with their opposite numbers, and the buyer (or seller) will generally discuss contractual issues with his or her own lawyer, who will relay points across. Anyone who has sold a house will tell you that part of the frustration occurs at the point when they are waiting for the lawyers to do their 'thing'. Progress appears slow, and when pushed, they have a tendency to blame the legal advisers of the other party. To avoid this situation, ensure that both sets of lawyers confirm their understanding of timescales and that a formal process for exchanging information is set.

The extent to which you communicate directly with the buyer will depend on the relationship you have with him or her. As a rule, the more things you resolve directly between yourselves the quicker matters will progress, but obviously you need to be careful to avoid agreeing to things that your lawyer might advise against.

I have often found lawyers to be poor communicators, and anyone who has sold a house will probably agree. Discuss communication at your initial meeting with legal advisers and make it clear to them that you value effective communication highly and expect to be fully informed at all points in the process.

Communicating with interested parties who are not directly involved in the transaction

The very nature of a business sale generally necessitates a high level of confidentiality. In most situations, employees and customers will not be informed of the sale until after completion. However, there will be situations when some people need to be involved earlier in the process. In terms of employees, the obvious example is in an MBO situation, but even then it is usually only the employees who are directly involved in the MBO (and will become shareholders) who will be aware of the sale. Ensure they sign confidentiality agreements. It could be the case that your buyer wants to talk to a number of key customers ahead of the sale. I would imagine that you will be very wary of this and you must think through all of the implications.

I have developed a general rule regarding communication in situations where confidentiality is important: 'Until you can tell everybody everything, don't tell anybody anything.' Consider adopting this as your starting point and only break the rule when you are clear as to the implications of doing so.

Post-completion communication with employees

Many of the people I spoke to who have sold businesses gave little thought to communicating with employees in the period following completion of the deal. People were basically told 'This has happened, I have put a few quid in the bank, thanks for your efforts, I'm off.' (Perhaps the actual words used were slightly more subtle, but this is the general thrust.) Our 'serial entrepreneur' told me that following the sale of his first business he communicated very little with employees (despite the fact that he stayed in the business for a couple of years), but took communication much more seriously during the second business disposal. We would do well to learn from his example.

People are basically self-centred when it comes to earning a living (including you and me) and employees immediately consider what's in it for them as soon as any kind of change is announced. Obviously, the sale of a business could be very positive – or negative – for specific employees, or employees in general depending on the circumstances of the sale. The simplest situation is when you sell to a party who will basically keep running the business as it is. In this situation, 'reassurance' is the key message for employees and they will want to know that their jobs, terms and conditions, working hours, and any environment will stay the same, or be made better. It has been suggested that speaking directly to employees in small groups, followed by written notification, is the best process to adopt, and it sounds like sensible advice. Of course this approach requires extra effort, but it might well be worth it. What I do know is, if you don't give people information they speculate to fill the gaps in knowledge, and sometimes the speculation can be both wildly inaccurate and dangerous for the business, as the following example demonstrates.

The receivers

Someone told me of a situation where communication issues caused enormous difficulties for a business that was being sold. The business was a construction company that was in very secret discussions with a much larger company that was interested in buying it. The situation would have been positive for all concerned, as the acquiring company had plans to expand into the specific sector that the smaller firm already operated in. However, over quite an extended period, many of the staff in the smaller firm noticed that small groups of people in stripey suits were 'crawling all over the business', asking questions and looking at invoices and other data. When challenged, the directors of the firm denied that anything was going on and said that the stripey suits were just auditors. Now people aren't stupid. They know that auditors arrive at the same time every year, and that they are usually quite discreet. The stripey suits had arrived in the wrong season and were not behaving like auditors should.

Knowing they were being lied to, and in the absence of any other information, rumours abounded and many members of staff concluded that the stripey suits were indeed receivers, or at least people sent by the bank because the business was in trouble. This was a reasonable conclusion given the lack of any other evidence. The rumours became so entrenched that three key staff dusted off their CVs and immediately received job offers from competitors. It will be no surprise to learn that these were the most important and experienced people in the business – after all, the best people are always in demand and find it easiest to secure other positions. Having three essential people hand in their notice in the space of a couple of weeks rocked the directors to the core, and the situation threatened the sale. The directors, in panic mode, had to take remedial action, offer higher salaries and become much more open as to what was going on.

My conclusion is that while it may be essential to maintain confidentiality, you cannot assume that people are stupid, and won't notice that things are happening. If you don't provide a believable story, they will make one (or several) up. The challenge is either to manage the process so tightly that people don't notice anything is happening, or develop a secure, positive and believable cover story. If this sounds like a strategic way of saying you might have to lie, I'm afraid that's exactly what it is.

In situations where the sale will lead to significant changes, the communication process will probably be led by the new owner. If jobs are to be lost, or premises relocated, a detailed consultation process will probably be required and it may be necessary to take legal advice – at least for the new owners. If the sale means significant changes for employees, the communication plan will need to be very carefully thought through.

Post-completion communication with customers

How will your customers respond to a change in ownership? Their response could well be anything from total lack of interest through to outrage, depending on your specific circumstances. It could be that you don't need to tell them anything, or you (and the new owner) might feel that a detailed explanation is required. In a few circumstances you may be contractually obliged to tell them, and if a formal agreement is in place they may even have the right to cancel your supply contract with them. They may never have heard of your buyer, which may worry them, or they may know your buyer very well indeed and hate them.

Even if you are walking away from your business with a cheque for 100 per cent of the sale value, you should still be concerned that the post-sale communication process with customers and employees is well managed and successful. After all, you will have given many warranties and indemnities in the share sale agreement (see Chapter 7) and some of these may be affected by the post-sale success of the business. Any new owner who unexpectedly loses major customers will not be happy and may look for ways of clawing money back from you.

Think carefully about what you communicate to whom (and how) when announcing the sale. And remember the golden rule of communication: it's not what you say, it's what they hear that counts.

KEEPING ON TRACK

You may have agreed that your solicitor will project manage the sale process on your behalf, and a good lawyer will be able to do this effectively. However, the success of the process is your responsibility. If the sale collapses in the latter stages, your lawyer will be paid most of his or her fees, and you will have no sale proceeds. However committed your lawyer, his or her motivation and reward are different to yours. The following points represent a few practical ideas for helping you keep on track.

Project plan

Draw up a simple project plan showing key activities to be completed. Be clear on timescales and who has responsibility for ensuring the activity is successfully completed. If all involved parties agree to the plan, it can be used (gently or otherwise) to point out when specific parties are falling behind the agreed timescales. An example project plan is included in Appendix A.

Regular briefings

Schedule regular briefings into your project plan. Perhaps this will involve a weekly telephone update with your lawyer, or a similar arrangement with the buyer. Discuss at the outset how you will keep in touch.

Confirm discussions

Picking up the phone is a quick, cheap and effective method of communication, but it is very transitory. Will you remember the details of a telephone conversation weeks later? More to the point, will your buyer? If you agree anything by telephone drop an e-mail (or brief written note) to involved parties confirming the salient points. Being disciplined in this respect can save a great deal of time and frustration later in the process.

Remain positive

From the discussions I have held with lawyers, accountants and business people, I can confirm that the process of selling a business is not always smooth and problem free. Lawyers on either side may uncover issues, or draft clauses that are frankly unacceptable to the other side. You may even find that an issue arises that makes your potential buyer 'wobble' and become uncertain whether to proceed (of course, this may well be a negotiation ploy). The best that you can do is to remain positive. Look for solutions not problems, and as a general rule 'Tell the other side what you can do, not what you can't do.'

Most business problems are surmountable with a little goodwill and a lot of enthusiasm, so ensure you carry both around with you at all times. There may be times when this is difficult, and on occasion you may be frustrated and stressed. I'm afraid that selling a business is one of those occasions when you are effectively being rewarded for feeling uncomfortable.

Chapter summary

▮ Managing the process is your responsibility. While professional advisers can help, you have by far the most to lose if things go awry. If the process goes wrong it will be your fault – or at least you will bear all of the consequences.

▮ Be organized ahead of time. The due diligence process will make many demands on your time. Tidy up the paperwork and keep records of all information shared.

▮ Have a well thought out plan for handling negotiations. Once the initial price negotiation is completed, you may feel the hard bit is over. It will have only just begun.

▮ Solicitors are notorious for having a 'single speed'. Ensure all parties agree to a firm timescale at the outset and do everything in your power to hold them to it.

▮ Think carefully about what you communicate, when and with whom. Be aware that just having unexpected 'stripey suits' in your business will communicate messages, even if they are unintended.

▮ Create a time plan and a communication plan (see Appendix A).

7

Legal Documentation

I once had a boss who, upon being presented with too much information, would bellow something along the lines of 'If it looks like an orange, and it feels like an orange, it's an orange. I don't want five pages of analysis just to prove it's a bleedin' citrus fruit.'

Wise words, and a philosophy business people might generally subscribe to. Lawyers, however, often take a very different perspective on life and their starting point might be more akin to:

> It certainly looks like an orange, but before you buy it we had better check its provenance, and ensure that the seller really does own the title. After all, you wouldn't want to buy a lemon, would you? And while we're at it, we had better test to see if insecticides have been used in the growing process, and we should also explore when and where it was picked. I wonder if they have an appropriate importation licence. We had better ask for a validated copy.

As you are *selling* a business, your own lawyer probably won't be so pedantic. But I'm afraid the buyer's lawyer almost certainly will. Questions such as 'is it theirs to sell?' and 'has it been properly maintained?' loom heavy in the lawyer's frame of reference. If what you are selling looks and feels like an orange, you will still have to prove beyond all reasonable doubt that the object is indeed a citrus fruit, of orange pigmentation.

Even if you own a relatively small and simple business the documentation accompanying the sale will be frustratingly complex. The level of complexity will be heavily influenced by the type of business you operate and the arrangements pertaining to the sale. This chapter does not claim to make you aware of the legal implications surrounding your sale, and you should always consult an appropriately qualified legal adviser. The purpose of this chapter is to make you aware of the type of issues that will be raised by lawyers advising both parties. It further aims to explain in broad (and generalized) terms some of the documentation that may be involved. Having reasonable knowledge may help you better understand some of the terminology used by your lawyer, and should help manage your interactions with him or her more effectively. Let us begin with a document that aims to limit what either party may do with confidential information that is disclosed as part of the sale process.

CONFIDENTIALITY AGREEMENT

The sale process necessitates confidential information being shared with your prospective buyer. In the early stages of your discussions this may be restricted to headline information covering turnover, profit and so on. As the sale process gathers pace, the information requirements will become very detailed. This will be forcibly established later in this chapter, when we cover the process called 'due diligence'.

It makes a great deal of sense to sign up to a detailed confidentiality agreement before disclosing any commercially sensitive information to any third party. You may have used confidentiality agreements in other aspects of your business life, but this is one situation where they are absolutely necessary. Basically, the agreement will state that certain proprietary information will be disclosed for the purpose of pursuing discussions relating to the potential sale and purchase of the business. The agreement goes on to define the different forms that this information may take and the obligations put on each party. You would be well advised to ask your solicitor to draw up a confidentiality agreement to ensure that you are properly protected. In outline, the agreement should take into account:

- the names and registered addresses of the contracting parties;
- a statement of the purpose for which the information may be used;
- a definition of what constitutes confidential information (which will be very broad, covering items such as papers, drawings, electronic files, financial documents and so on);
- the obligations of each party – in other words what you may or may not do with the information;
- restrictive clauses (for example, preventing the buyer from approaching any of your customers for a two-year period if the sale is not successfully concluded);

▌ 'delivering up', which is the lawyers way of saying that all information provided will be handed back or confirmed as destroyed upon a request from the other party;

▌ Broad contractual terms such as the agreement being interpreted under English law;

▌ signatures of all parties.

You will be well advised not to skimp on resources in creating a robust document.

For some businesses the information that needs to be disclosed may be very commercially sensitive indeed.

HEADS OF TERMS

Having signed a confidentiality agreement both parties (and any professional advisers involved at this stage) can begin the process of sharing information and discussing the potential deal. This will be the stage where major issues such as price and other key aspects of the sale are discussed. Let us assume that you agree an outline deal with your potential buyer. The first action is to write down the main points of the agreement. This document will become known as the 'heads of terms' (or 'heads of agreement') and will form the basis of more advanced contractual discussions. The document is not intended to bind either party to the sale, but it will probably include a number of clauses intended to enjoy contractual force. Such clauses may include a 'preferred bidder' agreement, where the seller grants exclusive negotiating rights to the potential buyer and puts any discussions with other bidders on hold. This is important to the buyer because the 'due diligence' phase of the process (detailed below) can be very expensive and require significant resources. The buyer does not want to invest time and resources if they may be gazumped at any stage in the process. Another common clause states that both parties will be responsible for the costs of their own professional advisers. It is unlikely that a potential buyer will be prepared to pick up your costs should the deal falter, and you should avoid any suggestions that you make any contribution to theirs.

The discussions that lead up to the agreement may be held with only the seller and potential buyer being present, but could also include professional advisers. You will not be surprised to learn that most account-ants and lawyers that I spoke to suggested it is essential to get professional advice and input at this key stage. If you don't do so, you may merely be delaying issues that need to be addressed until later in the process. Key points to focus on whilst creating the heads of terms document include, for example:

▌ Price: how will the price be calculated? If a formula is used it should be clearly stated and ideally an example calculation shown. What does the price depend upon? What factors may increase or reduce the price?

▌ Inclusions: for example, is stock included in the price, or will it be valued separately? If it is valued separately, how will this be done? What assets are included or excluded from the sale?

▌ Transition arrangements: will you be required to stay in the business? Will other key members of your management team? For how long?

▌ The number and type of shares included: some businesses have complex shareholdings. What about minority shareholdings? Do non-voting or other shares exist?

▌ The process to be followed to take the deal to completion: what happens next? Who does what? What timescales have been agreed? What happens if the sale falls through (refer back to confidentiality agreement).

▌ Creating an outline project plan (see the example in Appendix A).

Some aspects of the heads of agreement will necessarily remain woolly at this stage. For example, the buyer will wish to state that 'certain warranties and indemnities will be required from the seller' without necessarily stating what these are. Issues such as these will be explained in the next section on due diligence.

DUE DILIGENCE

Due diligence is a process rather than a document, but does involve the production of reams of documentation. The process is usually undertaken by a firm of accountants or solicitors (often both) on behalf of the buyer. The purpose of the process is to make extensive checks into any aspect of your business that may affect the buyer's desire to proceed with the purchase, or might influence the offer price. The buyer is looking to identify any risks that will affect future performance or profitability. They will also be keen to ensure that assets are actually owned outright, as opposed to being leased or financed in some other way. The process is analogous (in an over-simplified way) to paying for a full structural property survey and valuation before you buy a house. However, in the case of due diligence, the process may examine any number of aspects of your business, not just physical assets, and the process will be extensive, time-consuming and probably frustrating.

During the process you are required to provide 'full and fair disclosure' of all information requested. Obviously, you might be tempted to provide only partial information, or hold back on certain aspects; after all, doesn't the principle of *caveat emptor* (buyer beware) apply? Well, no. Making a limited (or even worse, false) disclosure is not a good idea, as later in the process you will probably be asked to provide indemnities and warranties against information that is either withheld or inaccurately disclosed. For example, if you know that a major customer has provided advance notification that it intends to terminate your supply contract, and this would have a significant impact on revenue or profits, you would be well advised to disclose the information. Why? Well, we could get into an ethical argument, but the legal position may well be that the buyer has recourse to pursue you for damages through a warranty or indemnity that you provided as part of the due diligence process. In any case, they will probably ask you to formally confirm whether any customers have advised that a contract will be terminated.

The due diligence process will be partly based on a thorough examination of hard information. This may include (but won't necessarily be limited to) the following:

- Historical audited accounts with particular emphasis on the balance sheet and profit and loss accounts.
- Current management accounts.
- Current business plan and financial forecasts (expect any assumptions to be tested).
- Leases and finance agreements.
- Supply agreements.
- Taxation paid or becoming due plus correspondence with revenue authorities.
- Bank statements (often requested directly from your bank – obviously requiring your express consent).
- Investments/capital assets (everything from buildings to IT equipment).
- Directors and employee employment contracts.
- Customer contracts.
- Health and safety records.
- Claims by employees (eg unfair dismissal).

▌ Compliance to statutory requirements (eg the offer of stakeholder pensions).
▌ Any other obligations or commitments.
▌ Stock.

In addition to hard data, less tangible or 'soft' information may be requested. This may include facilitating (confidential) discussions with customers or perhaps your accountant. They will also wish to understand the experience and skills of key staff and management. If you plan to exit the business rapidly, they will question how the business will function without you. They will consider how customers may react to your leaving. In fact they will consider any issue either internal or external that presents a risk to future profits and performance.

Keeping track of information supplied

The due diligence process is necessarily thorough and will extend over weeks or even months. By the end of it you may become confused as to what information was provided, to whom, when and in what format. For this reason you need to be organized – from the very beginning. It is a good idea to keep copies of everything you disclose and to store them in files along with any correspondence. Always disclose in writing if possible, as this will help avoid arguments later on. Your solicitor might advise that all information should be disclosed through themselves. Whatever approach you adopt, ensure that all information can be traced back to what was supplied and when. Also remember that should the process not lead to a sale, your confidentiality agreement allows you to instruct the other party to 'deliver up' all information supplied, or confirm in writing that all materials have been destroyed.

SHARE SALE AGREEMENT

The share sale agreement details exactly what the seller gets for his or her money.and covers the obligations of both parties in fine detail. Because each agreement is unique it is not possible to present a definitive list of inclusions here. However, it is likely that some or all the following will be included.

1. Parties to the agreement

This is an obvious point, but the document will need to clearly express who is involved in the transaction. You may be selling 100 per cent of your shares in a business, but several minority shareholders could be involved.

2. Interpretation/definitions

Lawyers expend a great deal of effort defining exactly what certain phrases mean and how they will be interpreted in the agreement. They have learnt by experience that the tighter the contract, the less opportunity for argument or legal challenge in the future. Expect even simple terms such as 'the business' or 'the directors' to be formally defined.

3. Warranties and indemnities

Warranties and indemnities are usually set out in detail within the share sale agreement and all lawyers will ensure their precise meanings are as tightly constructed as possible.

It may appear that the terms 'warranty' and 'indemnity' are interchangeable, but an experienced commercial lawyer advises that this is not the case.

Warranties

For a warranty to be effective, the buyer of your business would have to show that a breach in the warranty occurred, and that loss had been suffered as a consequence. For example, you might be asked to provide a warranty to the effect that a certain piece of equipment has been properly maintained, and confirm that you know of no reason that it will not continue to operate correctly. If the equipment breaks down six months after the new owner takes over, he or she may wish to pursue a claim against the warranty provided. For the claim to be successful he or she would have to demonstrate that the warranty had indeed been breached, and that loss had occurred. Your solicitor may argue that the equipment had been properly maintained up to the time of sale, and that you had no reason to suspect it would not continue to function successfully for many years. The key point is that although this claim may or may not be successful, you have a potential argument in defence and *the onus is on the buyer to prove that the warranty is effective and enforceable in this specific case.*

Indemnities

If we take the above example but change the position to a situation where you have given an indemnity, it might be that you offered to indemnify the seller against any repair or replacement costs for the machine in question for a period of, say, 12 months after the business sale is completed. If the equipment breaks down, it will simply have it fixed or replaced and send you the bill. The onus is now on you to demonstrate that the repair cost was due to direct damage that occurred after it had taken ownership. Perhaps a fork-lift tuck ran into the machine and the damage was therefore accidental and (hopefully) not included in the indemnity. *But the onus is now on you to demonstrate the indemnity is not operative.*

Clearly I have simplified the situation, and any experienced lawyer would ensure the warranty or indemnity is limited and clearly defined. However, in general, with an indemnity in force the seller will find it harder to defend the claim. You may be thinking that the optimum solution is to instruct your solicitor not to agree to any indemnities at all, and to use loosely-worded warranties instead. Sadly, the buyer has also employed an experienced lawyer and will have the opposite intentions in mind. It is a matter for negotiation, but you should at least be aware why it is worth investing time and effort in this area. By the way, all warranties and indemnities will be in force for a set timescale. Apparently one to three years is typical, but there will be certain issues that necessarily have a longer time-span. One example will be taxation, and you will probably be asked to provide a 'deed of covenant', which is an indemnity relating to all taxation issues that are not covered in the businesses accounts.

The specifics of each warranty and indemnity will probably be set out in a schedule at the end of the share sale agreement. Another important part of this document relates to the disclosure letter

4. The disclosure letter

The disclosure letter is your opportunity to disclose any information that might otherwise be the subject of a warranty or indemnity. I will use a simple example to demonstrate the principle.

Perhaps you are selling a delivery business and have been asked to provide a warranty to the effect that recorded mileage on all vehicles is accurate. If two of the vehicles were bought second-hand you really have no certain way of knowing that mileage is indeed accurate. You might want to include a note in the disclosure letter admitting that you cannot be certain as to mileage accuracy on these two vehicles. The information is now in the open and the buyer has the opportunity to factor this into negotiations. Having been disclosed, you would not be liable if it later emerged that one of the vehicles did indeed have inaccurate mileage recorded, unless of course you knew beforehand that the mileage was inaccurate, in which case you should have disclosed this fact ahead of time.

5. Consideration

This is lawyers' preferred term for 'money'. They may use a phrase such as 'The total consideration payable for the shares shall be £x (x pounds sterling) which will be payable on completion by bankers draft or CHAPS payment to the vendor's solicitors.'

6. Completion

This is the process by which the deal will be finalized. You might think completion is a case of, 'You give me the money and I will sign the shares over to you.' As ever, the process is more complicated. For example, where will completion take place? What documents will be served by each party? At the very least you will be required to formally hand over and sign share transfer documentation and share certificates at the completion meeting. Does the company require a final meeting of the board of directors? All of this requires agreement ahead of time, and the completion meeting is the place where details will be recorded and formalized.

7. Ongoing confidentiality requirements

Even if you are leaving the business immediately upon completion, it is likely that you will be bound not to disclose sensitive information about the company or the share sale transaction.

8. Covenants

These are restrictions on the parties and may be quite wide-ranging. For example, the seller may be asked to covenant that he or she will not work for, or hold shares in, a competitor business for a certain time period and/or within a specific geographical area. You may also be required to confirm that you will not poach staff from the business, and also undertake that you will not say or do anything to damage the organization's reputation.

9. General clauses

The 'general' section will include anything the lawyers deem important that is not covered elsewhere. For example, you may find a clause that sets out which country's legal system is to apply – of obvious importance if the buyer and seller operate in different countries.

One thing to beware of when considering any clause is 'too much generalization'. For example, one common clause might require a warranty that, 'There are no claims pending or threatened against the company by any employee which have not been formally detailed in the disclosure letter.' You might conclude that this sounds fair, especially if you have had the chance to disclose any claims that you are aware of. However, what if the clause were to read, 'There are no claims pending or threatened, *or capable of arising*, against the company by any employee.' How on earth do you know what is 'capable of arising'? You may conclude that the term is far too general – your solicitor should spot such terms and advise accordingly.

10. Schedules

Schedules set out the detail behind a number of clauses. For example, one schedule might contain and define all of the warranties and indemnities that have been agreed, and this may run to several pages. Another might detail the register of assets included in the sale.

OTHER IMPORTANT DOCUMENTS

If you are selling 100 per cent of your shares, most of the legal issues will be covered in the share sale agreement. But what if you are only selling some of your shares? You may remain a majority shareholder, or be left with just a minority holding. In either case, a separate shareholders agreement may be required. You may also remain within the company as an employee, and therefore a Service Agreement will have to be prepared. If you have sold part of your shares now, but have an agreement to sell the balance at some future date, an Option Agreement may be required. All of these additional documents are crucially important and deserve as much consideration as the obligations set out in the main share sale agreement.

Shareholders agreement

If you have sold part of your shareholding, the rights and responsibilities of all shareholders will need to be set out in detail. This is the primary purpose of the shareholders agreement. The general format will be similar to the share sale agreement, and the parties to the agreement and definitions will probably be found at the front of the document. The agreement may be wide ranging and could include factors such as the following.

The constitution of the company

This may address questions such as 'Who will sit on the board of directors?', 'Who is entitled to have representation on the board?', 'How will shareholders' rights be assigned?' and 'What is the necessary quorum for transaction of business at board level?'

The conduct of the company's affairs

What rights does each shareholder have to examine management accounts? Who will appoint the auditors? How often will board meetings be held? These are examples of important questions that require consideration. The key point is that any shareholder who is not directly involved in running the business needs to have his or her investment protected. For example, perhaps you previously held 100 per cent of the company's shares but sold 75 per cent of them in a management buy out and no longer wish to work within the business. What steps would you wish to take to ensure the business continues to operate profitably? Perhaps you would want to nominate someone to sit on the board to look after your interests. Beyond this you may also wish to specify limits on decisions that can be taken without a formal vote of shareholders. This may include things like the acquisition of property, or other major capital assets. Also, you may think it important to put limits on the amount by which directors' salaries can be increased without referral to all shareholders.

If you plan to remain a shareholder in a business you no longer directly manage, you should discuss issues such as the above with your legal adviser as early in the process as possible.

Option agreement

You may have sold only part of the shares in your business at the present time, but have a firm agreement to sell the balance at a future date. This might be based, perhaps, on some profit-driven formula. In this situation the lawyers will prepare an option agreement.

The purpose of the option agreement is to set out in fine detail what rights the buyer has to purchase the rest of the shares and the value that will be paid. It will also specify the time frame that the transaction will be completed within and the specific circumstances that will apply.

Service agreement

If you are remaining in the business as a director you will probably be required to sign a service agreement. This is very analogous to a contract of employment, but as you are (probably) seen as being crucial to the future success of the business, the terms might be very detailed and quite onerous. As is usual in all legal documentation, you will probably find that the terms are tightly defined at the front. The document may also cover key aspects of your employment, such as:

▌ duties incumbent on the role you are fulfilling;
▌ remuneration and benefits;
▌ holidays and other entitlements;
▌ rules and conditions pertaining to terminating the agreement;
▌ sickness and other procedures;
▌ confidentiality;
▌ external business interests;
▌ various restrictions (for example limiting your ability to work for competitors for a fixed time after the agreement has been terminated);
▌ ownership of intellectual property;
▌ general terms.

Compromise agreement

In contrast to the service agreement covering your remaining in the business, you may be leaving immediately and resigning as a director. In this situation you may be asked to sign a compromise agreement which limits your ability to make future claims against the business as an ex-employee. This is a very important document because it asks you to waive a number of rights – some of which are enforceable by statute. For this reason the document will probably have to be countersigned by your solicitor, who will have explained the implications of the various clauses to you. You may be asked to agree to waive a variety of rights, including claims for:

▌ pay in lieu of notice or damages for terminating employment without the necessary notice;
▌ holiday or sick pay;
▌ any outstanding bonuses, overtime or other form of remuneration;
▌ unfair dismissal;
▌ sex, age, race or disability discrimination;
▌ redundancy payment;
▌ any other claims against the business relating to your employment.

Of course, you may have been handsomely rewarded for selling your business and waiving these rights is not necessarily unreasonable.

Lease assignment document

If your business is a limited company and the property lease is held by the company, the lease is technically not changing hands, and will not need to be assigned. If the lease is in your name, however, and you plan to pass on liability for the lease (assuming this is allowed under the terms of the lease agreement), lawyers will prepare a document for this purpose. This document effectively passes ownership from the seller to the buyer. However, this does not necessarily pass all liability to the buyer. The 'retail' section of Chapter 8 explains more about the complex topic of property leases.

Licence to assign

Assuming the lease agreement allows the lease to be assigned to a third party (the general rule is that your landlord cannot 'unreasonably withhold permission'), a document entitled 'licence to assign' will need to be prepared for signature by the landlord.

Your business may have important leases other than those relating to property. Machinery is often leased. Even the humble photocopier is leased rather than purchased. All leases will need to be submitted as part of the due diligence process and assignment documents may need to be prepared for each of them.

Articles of association

The articles of association is a statutory legal document required by all limited companies. The articles set out the internal rules that govern the powers and responsibilities of the officers of the company (directors and company secretary). The articles may need to be rewritten depending on the circumstances of your sale.

Meeting minutes

Important activities such as the removal or appointment of directors or the transfer of shares will need to be approved at a formal board meeting, the minutes of which must be written up and saved in a formal register. Your final act as a director may be to formally resign from the company and this must be recorded. The minutes will usually be approved at the completion meeting when the sale is finally implemented.

DOCUMENT PREPARATION

Which side should prepare the legal documentation: the buyer's or seller's legal advisers? It is more likely that the buyer will wish to instruct his or her own solicitors to create the first draft as the document aims to protect his or her interests after you have disappeared with the cash. Having said that, if you are only selling part of your shareholding and plan to remain in the business (or have some kind of buyout from profit arrangement) it may be you who is looking to include the maximum range of 'defensive' clauses. Obviously whichever side creates the documentation has greater control over the structure, but they will face a bigger bill for legal services.

By necessity this chapter has only been able to skim across a very complex range of topics. Hopefully you will now be better able to quickly understand the importance of a range of documents that will be prepared by lawyers in the course of the sale.

Chapter summary

▌ Ensure that you enjoy the protection afforded by confidentiality agreements.

▌ Create a 'heads of terms' document early in the process. One lawyer advised that doing so 'saves time, confusion and cost'.

▌ The due diligence process will be detailed and probably frustrating. Ensure you keep track of all information and documents disclosed. Be efficient at administration during this period.

▌ The share sale agreement is a crucially important document. Pay particular attention to warranties and indemnities.

▌ If you are only selling part of your shareholding, a shareholders agreement may well be required between you and the other parties.

▌ If you are selling part of your shareholding now but have agreed a fixed date to sell the balance, the details will be covered by an option agreement.

▌ If you are to continue working in the business after the sale you should ensure a service agreement is created.

▌ When leaving the business, a compromise agreement might be required, which forbids claims for unfair dismissal or other employment-related matters.

▌ Always employ the services of an experienced commercial solicitor.

8

Advice for Specific Sectors

Businesses can be considered to be, as the saying goes, 'The same, only different.' One of the difficulties in making this book genuinely useful is the sheer diversity in what constitutes a business. For all I know you could be looking to sell your pistachio nut importing business or an ice-cream van in Wolverhampton. If asked whether the sale process for both is the same I would have to mutter 'Well, yes, kind of, but different.'

Your business will be unique. Even if you operate a franchise it is unlikely that your business exactly replicates another. At the very least *you* are different from other franchisees and, as we know, businesses are about people. This chapter reflects on the issues underpinning this uniqueness, with the objective of exploring how the business sale might be affected by the sector you operate within.

FACTORS THAT MIGHT AFFECT THE SALE

You don't have to work in the food industry to know that pistachio nuts and icecreams are not the same. Yes, of course, one is cold and soft, and the other is round and hard. Nuts grow on trees and icecream grows in factories. Aside from the obvious physical attributes, market sectors have a range of characteristics that add a level of uniqueness to the nature of the business, and of course these factors can significantly influence why someone would want to buy a business in that sector. Before focusing on a number of sectors by way of example, it may be useful to reflect on some of the characteristics involved.

Customers

Some businesses sell directly to the public. Others sell to businesses. Some sales are small (icecream to children), others are very large (houses to their parents). Some products lend themselves to repeat sales, and others are one-offs (icecream and houses, again).

Contractual relationships

In addition to the above characteristics, the contractual relationship is important. The ice-cream van has no formal written contractual relationship with customers, but this is not true will all small purchases. You may have a formal contract for magazine subscriptions (and a direct debit payment), despite the fact that the product only costs a few pounds.

Product properties

Some products have a short shelf-life; think fresh cream cakes or newspapers. If your business sells these you will need to have a pretty good handle on volumes, and extremely effective distribution arrangements. Other products can sit in a warehouse for years. Factors like this can affect the level of knowledge and experience required to successfully run a business in a specific sector, and may affect the attractiveness of your business to new entrants into the market.

Seasonality

Linked to product property is seasonality. Some products are extremely seasonal. Growing strawberries in the United Kingdom springs to mind, as does selling buckets and spades in Blackpool. Other products are only pseudo-seasonal, for example Easter eggs or Christmas cards. In both of these examples similar products (chocolate and birthday cards) can be produced all year round.

Supply market

Icecream is not a naturally occurring product, but nuts are. Icecream can be pretty much produced at will, and in fluctuating volumes. Nuts grow, and you get what you get. Of course, you can plant more nut trees and (for all I know) increase the yield by effective management, but nature always has the upper hand. Many factors influence the nature of the supply market to your business.

Capital

Some businesses require relatively little capital and others a great deal. Some have huge amounts of fixed capital tied up in machinery, land and property. Others require relatively little. Some businesses require lots of fluid working capital to pay workers until revenue grows large and regular enough to cover costs. I guess that software development businesses might fall into this category.

People

Businesses in some sectors require very highly skilled people. Most forms of engineering would fall into this category. Others require large numbers of low-cost, relatively low-skilled workers to be successful. Early on in my career I was given responsibility for improving contract cleaning in the large supermarket group that I worked in. In this scenario, achieving high standards required literally thousands of low-paid workers to turn up each day at strange times, and do relatively physical or unpleasant jobs. Unsurprisingly, absenteeism and staff churn are very high in this situation. Ever since then I have felt that running a contract cleaning business requires a certain type of person to be successful.

Competitors

The competitive nature of markets is in constant flux, and economists tell us that where there is insufficient competition, more will quickly develop – at least if there are profits to be made. Your business may be in a relatively new sector, eg software engineering, or a very old established one such as contract cleaning. The competitive nature of the market, and barriers to entry, will be an important factor to consider.

All of the above combine to tell you something about the relative attractiveness of certain sectors, and help you think about who might be interested to buy and why. Examples of a small number of sectors are considered below.

CONSULTANCY

There has been a huge explosion of businesses defined as 'consultancies' in recent years. The Institute of Business Consulting has thousands of members and is growing year on year. And of course there are many other types of consultant that don't link with the word 'management'. Think of any sector, from agriculture to politics to railways, and you will find speciality consultancy businesses generating revenue from involvement in innumerable projects. Many, perhaps most, large organizations utilize people on a consultancy basis, whether in the public sector (the government is constantly criticized for the huge amounts spent on consultants) or the private sector.

If we consider the factors mentioned above in relation to consultancy, the insights are quite interesting:

▮ Customers: tend to be large organizations (rarely individuals).
▮ Contractual relationships: formal contracts, usually of fixed duration.
▮ Product property: service-based, usually relates to solving a single problem.
▮ Seasonality: not usually a major factor, depending on the customer's sector.
▮ Supply market: depends on the speciality of the consultant.
▮ People: generally highly skilled, experienced specialists.
▮ Competitors: becoming increasingly competitive and specialized.

Overall, consultancy requires people to have strong selling skills to sell at a high level into large organizations. Specific skills and experience in the subject in question are also crucial. Sales tend to be project-based rather than highly repetitive, and therefore generating regular work is a challenge. Most consultancy markets are becoming more competitive. If you have the skills to enter a particular sector the barriers to entry are low – you only need a suit, laptop, business cards and means of transport, and you're in business. This begs the question: if you were the kind of person who could set up a consultancy business, why buy one? This leads us onto the key issue surrounding the sale of a consultancy-based organization: is it a real 'stand-alone business', or just a few self-employed people operating under the banner of a broader organization?

Companies, self-employment and virtual businesses

Many consultancy businesses are effectively 'one-man-bands', but are nevertheless fully incorporated limited companies. This is one reason why it is difficult to determine the 'real businesses' from the single-person self-employed. Why is this differentiation important? Well, from a business-sale perspective there is quite a difference between a lone person who earns a living by selling his or her time, and a fully functioning company with premises, employees and well-established medium-term contracts. One may have value beyond the individual, but the other almost certainly will not. A couple of brief case studies may help confirm the key differences.

The virtual organization

Liz Ellis and Michael Clark jointly run a successful consultancy business from an office in the garden of their home in North Yorkshire. The pair have different skills and, as a general rule, different customers, though on occasion the opportunity arises to work together on a single project. The key theme of the business is 'communication' and under this heading they provide a variety of services, from training platform speakers how to communicate more effectively, right through to organizing major events involving hundreds of people. Running a major event is not easy when you are restricted to the resources of only two people. However, they ascribe much of their success to the clear strategy of being a 'virtual organization', and in fact use this approach as a key selling point with potential customers. They have a very broad range of contacts and when working on major projects draw on many other 'self-employed' people like themselves, but who have other skills. So, when organizing a major event they may need the services of a video crew, stage designers, lighting engineers and so on. Being a virtual organization has an obvious advantage: very low overheads. Unlike traditional employees, none of the aforementioned video crew, etc is being paid when not working, and they do not have to be provided with expensive equipment and workspace. The approach works well for their consultancy business, because it is the best way of delivering high value to customers.

The downside to the virtual organization is that it is difficult to identify any value that would appeal to a potential buyer. In the case of EllisClark Associates, all of the value in the business lies in the skill and experience of the two principals, and anyone considering buying the business would immediately realize this. However, Michael Clark is happy to accept the fact that his business will never be saleable, and confirms 'The virtual organization works for us. It is a vehicle for earning our living doing something we enjoy. At the outset we agreed a clear strategy that involved no employees, and no expensive premises. On this basis we have to accept that although our business revenue may grow year on year, we are not developing the asset value of the business, and it would never be attractive to a prospective purchaser. It's a shame because it would obviously be nice to sell up and pocket some cash one day, but you can't have it all ways.'

Does this example imply that consultancy businesses are never attractive? Obviously not. First, if you have a consultancy with a larger number of employees, which has both physical assets and processes that ensure the business will keep generating revenue and delivering profits, your business may be very attractive to potential purchasers. Secondly, you may be a small consultancy-type business that has secured medium- or long-term supply contracts, which may be of significant interest to other organizations. In fact, my own business developed along these lines.

Managed services

As with the EllisClark Associates case study, my own business began as a partnership between two people who set up with the objective of being 'self-employed'. The two of us worked on consultancy projects for leading organizations, and although some customers provided opportunities of work on an ongoing basis, we were basically 'jobbing consultants'. The business had no value from an external perspective. However, an opportunity arose to outsource a specific service required by one of our clients and we agreed a two-year deal to provide a managed service under a formal contract. This meant recruiting two employees and taking a small office. Two things were now different. First, we had a guaranteed two-year revenue stream (obviously subject to delivering a high-quality service) and secondly, we had developed a kind of 'product', which was a unique method of managing a specific business requirement. Having set up an office, we thought it might be a good idea to try to replicate the solution and offer it to other organizations, which we duly did with some success. Soon we had three medium-term contracts and had developed our service into something unique that could be described to others. By this stage about 75 per cent of revenue came from these contracted services, with only 25 per cent being generated by consultancy. The business now had potential value, and indeed two larger organizations expressed an interest in buying our shares.

It is possible (and accurate) to argue that the business was no longer a 'consultancy' in the true sense, although part of the value to other organizations was the intellectual capital that exists in a consultancy-type business. The point to make for people who run a consultancy business but would like to grow its potential sale value is to identify medium- to long-term revenue streams and/or develop a very specific 'product' that is of value to others but is difficult to replicate. If I am being honest, we stumbled on this by accident rather than design. Having business strategies is a fine approach, but sometimes real life just throws up an opportunity!

SERVICE BUSINESSES

A lawyer recently said to me that valuing a service business is difficult because its main assets (ie its people) could simply walk out of the door. While I understand the point, I think it requires a heavy qualification, and is far too simplistic. The value of a business depends on many more things than just 'people'. Perhaps a very small service business (for example a consultancy as described above) is at risk of its main value being locked into the heads of just a few people, but surely this does not really apply on a larger scale. Think of Google, currently valued at literally hundreds of times its post-tax profits, yet it is in essence a service business. Yes, it has significant physical assets, but the value of the business is not really linked to them. The value of Google lies in its pre-eminent position in internet services and the expectations of its future prospects. In fact, if you take a look at share prices for publicly quoted companies it appears that service businesses are often preferred by investors.

The list of factors detailed at the beginning of this chapter suggest that as well as considering the people in the business we must reflect on many other important considerations. Who are the customers of the service business? What is the nature of the contractual relationship between them? What are the specific properties of the service provided? Can this service be 'packaged' to in effect become a product in itself? (If your business is car valeting – which is a service – could you realistically call the resulting product a 'clean car'? I believe this is valid.).

Hopefully you get the idea that considering all of the important factors noted above (and others that may occur to you) will help in determining the best approach in your sector. In essence, I believe the most important factors in relation to many service businesses relate to:

▮ Agreeing medium-term contracts with a reasonably broad customer base.
▮ Developing operating models and processes that create some level of uniqueness and allow you to demonstrate that a finished 'product' is delivered.

- Recruiting and looking after key staff – find ways to lock them in.
- Using PR techniques to develop your reputation and brand (see Chapter 5).

RETAIL

One very important matter that is often relevant to retail businesses relates to property leases. (As with all parts of this book relating to complex legal matters, the advice here is for general guidance purposes. Leases are complicated and important documents. Always speak to a lawyer before taking any action with regard to leases.)

Many independent retailers work out of leased premises. As location is a vital factor for this kind of business, most retailers sign up to long-term lease agreements extending to 10, 15, even 25 years. Doing so obviously affords a reasonable level of security. However, there is a serious downside in agreeing a long-term lease: you are absolutely obliged to meet the terms of the lease whatever happens to your business. If you haven't examined your lease agreement recently, you might think that selling your business transfers liability for the lease to the buyer, but (unless your have negotiated a very favourable arrangement) this is unlikely to be the case. Two types of clause typically cause the problem.

Continuing liability

The concept of continuing liability is based on the principle that when you assign (pass on) your lease to another party (the person or firm buying your business), if they default on payment (or other terms) you will still be liable. For example, if you sell your business with five years to run on the lease, and the new owner goes bust after a year, you retain liability for the lease for the following four years, even though you might have retired and considered your money to be safely stored in the bank. If your business is a limited company, it might be that the company (rather than yourself) is the party to the lease, and therefore when you sell all of the shares your liability passes to the new shareholders. However, if you had to provide a personal guarantee within the lease agreement you will retain liability. This leads to the second important clause to look out for.

Guarantor liability

It is easy to set up a limited company. Doing so affords a great deal of protection for the shareholders. When a limited company is wound up the general principle is that its liabilities cease to exist. For this reason, most landlords will require the shareholders (and/or directors) in the business to provide personal guarantees against the lease. This means that if your company (or its new owners if you have sold it) don't pay the rent, you have to. The effect is the same as described above under 'Continuing liability'.

While the above two clauses represent the general principle of liability when assigning leases, the Landlord and Tenants (Covenants Act) 1995, which came into force on 1 January 1996, changed the liability that tenants have under a lease.

Leases entered into after 1 January 1996 usually contain provisions that enable the landlord to call upon the outgoing tenant to sign an 'authorized guarantee agreement'. This is an agreement whereby the outgoing tenant guarantees the performance of the incoming tenant *but this applies for one assignment only*. This means that if the lease is assigned again (your buyer assigns to someone else), then the liability under the authorized guarantee agreement ends automatically.

In addition to the above Act, a voluntary code exists relating to business leases, which is supported by many leading property professionals and industry bodies representing both landlords and tenants. The Code for Leasing Business Premises in England and Wales, 2007, aims to promote fairness in commercial leases, and recognizes a need to increase awareness of property issues, especially among small businesses.

Sometimes a lease will utilize 'rent deposits' instead of personal guarantees. For example, you might have paid a deposit extending to six months rent to the landlord. If you sell the business and assign the lease to the new owners, the landlord will usually not be required to hand back the deposit. The idea is that he or she retains the deposit until the lease expires. This needs to be factored into your sale agreement, as you will probably wish to ask your buyer to pay you a sum equivalent to the six months' deposit. They would then get this back from the landlord when the lease finally expires.

MANUFACTURING

Manufacturing businesses tend to face the same difficulties as other organizations – plus a few more. As always, this does of course depend on the specific sector. If you run a manufacturing business, characteristics other than the fact that you make things will probably be more relevant to the 'saleability' of your company.

Specific problems faced by manufacturers relate to the need for high levels of capital investment: having predictable demand; attracting, recruiting and employing significant numbers of staff, and cheaper competitors that produce in parts of the world that have much lower labour costs and less compliance with health and safety requirements. Just thinking about these issues makes me wonder who would want to run a manufacturing business in the United Kingdom – and the answer is fewer and fewer people. However, while it is true that Britain produces fewer high-volume consumer products (say cars or televisions) than many other parts of the world, many smaller manufacturing business continue to do well.

Specific advice for manufacturing businesses is uncannily similar to that for service businesses. Try to spread the customer base. Have formal contracts. Invest time and effort into developing a brand, and formalize processes so that the business would continue if key people leave or fall under a bus. In addition to these generic points there is a specific issue that must be addressed. Given the increasing levels of international competition, and the lower wage rates enjoyed by producers in many countries, does the business have a long-term future in UK-based production? Clearly the answer to this question involves understanding the market that the company serves. It also involves contemplating whether the value of your product is driven by efficiency or flexibility.

Efficiency or flexibility

In many walks of life we find a trade-off between what is low cost and efficiently produced, and receiving flexibility or diversity. For example, if Ford produced just one type of car, it could be sold much more cheaply than having a whole range of different models, sizes, colours and fuel types. But not everyone wants the same car. The principle applies in similar ways to a range of different products. Take printed materials. Most of the medium volume commercial colour print that is bought by, say, UK-based insurance companies, is produced in the United Kingdom. Why? Because a very wide range of products are required in relatively small runs, and speed of turnaround is important. The insurance companies want suppliers that are relatively local and very flexible. Good news for the UK-based commercial printers. However, if you run a printing business that specializes is very high volume standardized printed products, you will be faced with increasing levels of international competitors. In this scenario, it makes sense for the customer to focus on high-efficiency, low-cost production techniques.

The same applies in many other sectors. Take clothing and fashion. Chic 'high-fashion', low-volume clothing sold in UK boutiques is often produced relatively locally. But very high-volume and low-cost products tend to be produced in the Far East. The key point from the perspective of someone selling a UK manufacturing business is to consider the efficiency versus flexibility angle, and ensure it is properly encapsulated in the sale memorandum.

Chapter summary

▌ Your business may be unique, but it shares many characteristics with other organizations.

▌ Think about the factors that might affect the sale *from the buyer's viewpoint.*

▌ Different types of business face a different mix of challenges. Ensure you are clear about the key issues surrounding the sale of your business.

9

Golden Handcuffs: Surviving a 'Lock-In' Period

A buyer has emerged, lawyers and accountants have advised, and after much frustration contracts are signed and the cheque banked. Are you on a sunny beach eating lobster and drinking chilled Möet? I didn't think so.

If you have sold anything other than a very simple business, or have arranged an MBO, there is a strong chance that the new owners will wish to retain your expertise, at least for a period. If they appointed an experienced lawyer they will probably have deferred part of your pay-off and perhaps linked it to ongoing profitability. How do you feel about this? All kinds of reactions are possible. You may be thrilled at the prospect of working with the new owner. Perhaps you have sailed single-handed for too long and welcome the opportunities for support. Maybe your business has been bought by a larger organization and you have picked up a broader role with new challenges. Perhaps the cheque in the bank has released pressures from other parts of your life; the mortgage on your house has been paid off or school fees settled for the coming years. Alongside these positive aspects there may well be negatives, which may only exist inside your head, but this is a very dangerous place to store them. At least, it is a place where they can cause a great deal of angst. Some problems are practical, but others more emotional. Examples from the latter category occur simply because what used to be yours is now someone else's and you feel differently about it. Practical problems can arise for a whole raft of reasons, some important and others seemingly trivial. The trivial may irritate you the most. A few examples are set out below to help you think through how you would handle the various situations that may materialize.

BIG DECISIONS ARE NOW SHARED DECISIONS

Previously, when you wanted to make a new appointment or buy an additional piece of machinery, you just did it. Now you have to seek approval before acting. This is as much a psychological issue as anything else. Having set up and run a business for several years, you have metamorphosized into a different animal; one that is used to taking decisions on a daily basis and living with the consequences. Having to seek approval from a 'boss' can feel a lot like, well, going back to school. 'Please sir, I need the toilet.' 'Why didn't you go at break time Jenkins? Now sit back down and shut up.'

NEVER EXPLAIN OR JUSTIFY

Running your own business means that generally speaking you don't have to explain or justify your actions to anyone else. This is not meant to sound aggressive, and clearly there will be many times when things are fully explained to staff, customers or suppliers. But it is your choice. Now you may find that accounts are poured over each month and you have to formally explain – and justify – what is going on within the business. Most large organizations operate within such formal process-driven rules, but smaller business tend to avoid this approach because it somewhat bureaucratic and time-consuming. The Japanese have a wonderful term for people who work for large organizations – the 'salaryman'. If your business has been bought by a large organization and you now work in it, you have morphed into such an object (or at least a 'salaryperson').

SMALL FACTORS BECOME ANNOYING

You know how previously you scrawled monthly expenses down on a sheet of A4 and asked your payroll person to make out a cheque? Not any more. A new form written in Microsoft Excel (which contains macros and pivot tables) needs to be filled in by the 21st of the month ('I'm sorry Mr Smith, we need them on the 21st. Not a week before and certainly not a week after. We can't have anarchy in the accounts office now, can we Mr Smith?') Six months later you have still failed to claim any expenses and are now in trouble because the accounts team are having to accrue a figure to cover their debt to you.

Other people's processes, however sensible and well-intentioned they may be, are just too annoying to handle. Be prepared to live with it. No one has ever successfully challenged the bureaucratic aspirations of the accounts department.

THE HUMAN RIGHTS ACT

The negatives surrounding a lock-in may equally count as positive. For example, you may genuinely welcome improved processes that are being implemented by the new owner. Perhaps they represent things you would have done had you not been so busy making money.

One area where you may be particularly pleased to have a problem shared, and therefore at least halved, is in the area of managing people. Employing people is becoming increasingly difficult, and risky – especially for smaller businesses. Governments (of the local, national and European varieties) appear to imagine that all businesses have professionally staffed HR teams. Well, this is not going to be the case if you run a butcher's shop with five employees, two of whom are part-time. Despite the modest size of your butcher's shop, and the difficulty in making a profit when four major supermarkets operate within a five-mile radius, the government will burden you to the same extent they do Tesco. You will have to offer your staff a pension, and handle any extracurricular payments they have to make such as 'child support'. For your own protection you will be forced to create and adopt written policies relating to discipline, equal opportunities, disability, maternity leave, appraisals and promotion, and many other topics that governments of one kind or another think is the job of the small business person. Of course you have to do this on top of being the government's VAT, PAYE and general tax collector.

Many of the above government-led initiatives do of course have noble intentions. Creating fair opportunities for the disabled or ensuring pregnant women aren't discriminated against are objectives that should enjoy broad support. But they are far too complex to be handled by unsupported small business owners (on top of everything else a business has to do such as turning a profit and looking after customers). The Human Rights Act and the discrimination acts are a minefield. I certainly don't understand them, and it appears that many professionals who operate in the HR field don't either – at least not with conviction. Frankly, and speaking from experience, it was a great relief to get help in these areas when the larger firm that bought my business offered assistance through a qualified HR team.

For me, the worst part of running a business is employing people. And it isn't the fault of the employees. It is the fault of government. Think I'm being too hard on government? Recently a man who had written and self-published a local history book asked if it could be stocked in his local library and Town Hall reading room. 'Yes,' came the reply, 'as long as you can provide £5 million of public liability insurance.' When pushed to explain this ludicrous demand, he was advised that his book could potentially fall on someone's head, or readers could suffer a paper cut. This is how the public sector operates – and why I never work within it. I rest my case.

IDEAS FOR A SUCCESSFUL LOCK-IN

For many people, the ideal scenario will be to leave the business quickly, allowing just enough time for an effective handover and proper communications with staff, customers, suppliers and (my least favourite business-speak group) other stakeholders. If this is not possible or indeed practical, the following may help you plan for and manage your lock-in period a little more successfully.

The serial entrepreneur

Following the sale of his first business, Tony Gill was effectively 'locked-in' to the plc that had acquired his business. His emotions at this time were mixed. Partly he felt relief that the stressful sale process (which had taken nine months) was over, and he had money in the bank that would guarantee his family's financial future. His other emotion was one of 'bereavement'. As he says, 'The business now belonged to someone else, and I no longer felt the same about it.' Interestingly, staff who he had worked with on a friendly basis for many years changed their attitude towards him. They became distant. Was this as a result of his financial status? Perhaps the fact that he was no longer the 'boss'? Tony isn't sure as to the reasons but he is clear that things were different.

Throughout the lock-in period he continued to work hard – putting in long days and contributing to the ongoing success of the wider business. Although his relationship with the directors of the acquiring business was good, he struggled to come to terms with the idea of having a boss. 'All of a sudden, after many years in charge, I now reported in to someone. This was very difficult to handle. I continued to work hard, but didn't really feel happy or comfortable.' The result of this discomfort was that as soon as he could contractually leave the business he did so. The lock-in wasn't working.

This all happened many years ago, but the effect has stayed with Tony to the present day, and heavily influenced his thinking when he recently sold his second business. In Chapter 6 I wrote about how Tony had developed relationships with his European competitors. In 2005 one of them made a very attractive offer to buy all of the shares in his business, for a very large sum, in cash. Unfortunately there was a caveat: a five-year lock-in period. The valuation wasn't a problem but the lock-in was. He could not countenance a further extended period in a business he no longer owned, so he decided to explore other options.

He approached the businesses bank manager and discussed the idea of the bank funding a management buyout on behalf of the existing management team. Tony realized this would have to be made attractive to both the bank and the management team, so he put forward a significant discount on the offer he already had on the table from Europe. His payback for providing the discount would be the chance to exit the business immediately on completion of the sale. After all, the existing team was already in place to continue the success of the business. A good solution all round it seems. However, it is worth noting that the discount that Tony was prepared to offer was a very substantial sum. Enough for you or me to live on in some comfort for the rest of our lives – and he gave it away. When I asked how I justified this course of action to himself, he simply replied 'It was the money versus five years of my life. I already have enough money to live on, so why would I want more in exchange for five years that I would never get back?' A nice example which proves the maxim that time really is money.

Set a specific period

If you plan to stay in and develop the business long term (without a fixed period agreement) you are not really in a lock-in situation. Nevertheless, you may still have an extended employment contract, perhaps committing you to a one-year termination period. Think very carefully about what you sign up to, as you will need to honour this agreement for both ethical and legal reasons. Remember to consider how your feelings towards the business and your role within it might change soon after the sale. Chapter 7 considers employment contracts and other formalities relating to being 'locked-in'.

For those facing a 'traditional' fixed-term lock-in of one, two or three years, consideration needs to be given to the optimum duration. My advice would be, the shorter the better, but commercial considerations need to be taken into account. If your buyer is very keen to lock you in for three years, he or she will probably aim to include financial incentives – and penalties – in both your employment contract and the share sale agreement. It is worth pushing back on any agreement that significantly constrains you in the future. Obviously the extent to which you push back, or capitulate, will depend on your circumstances. Just be aware of the future consequences when agreeing to longer-term commitments. Once, many years ago, I was about to sign a five-year agreement with a supplier. A solicitor asked me 'What will happen in five years? How will your business look? What will its needs be?' Of course I couldn't really see five years ahead, and said so. 'Fine,' she advised, 'so don't agree to any five year contracts with suppliers.' Good advice that I have never forgotten. If it applies to suppliers it should certainly apply to someone wishing to buy your company.

Get cash up front

I am reiterating a point made earlier, but the more cash up front that can be agreed the better. Where possible, avoid being paid out of future profits from the business – especially if they are 100 per cent yours now.

Set the ground rules

Let us assume you have agreed to stay in your (sold) business for a further two years. What can you do to ensure a good working relationship and successful outcome? Agree the ground rules up front. Surprises are best avoided when it comes to business relationships. Setting the ground rules needn't be acrimonious; in fact in can help you and the new owner of your business to understand each other better. In setting the rules you should consider factors such as:

▮ how general administration will change – expenses, billing, salaries and so on;

- what your key responsibilities will be – perhaps sales growth, client management and profitability;
- financial rewards – payment of bonuses and so on (which should be encapsulated in your contract of employment);
- reporting lines – who you will report to; how reporting lines will change for existing staff;
- the limits of your authority – can you still sign cheques? Agree to leases? Make staff appointments without approval? Ideally much of this will be set out in your contract of employment, but some things will occur that were not considered at the time agreements were being put together;
- integration – if your business has been bought by a larger organization, what aspects will be integrated into the parent company? Perhaps you will share a common finance team or HR department. Major issues such as these must be addressed early in your discussions with the buying organization;
- meetings – you may consider this a trivial point, but what meetings will you be required to attend and with whom? If you have been acquired by a larger organization, what access do you have to its managing director? Will you schedule regular meetings?

Pass the things you don't like

Don't tell anyone I suggested this, but this could be the time to drop responsibilities or tasks that you don't like. Are you fed up with being directly responsible for managing everyone? Do you hate handling finance? Do you a have a customer you could gladly throttle? Find a good reason to lose one or two things that you currently don't like doing, and look on it as part of the overall reward package.

Focus your efforts

If you are financially incentivized to keep growing the business (and profitability) you should allocate as much time as possible doing things that support that specific objective. After all, selling is the only activity that brings in revenue. Everything else just adds cost. What will be the key success factors that ensure a profitable and mutually happy exit in two years' time? Ensure that you new job description (and contract of employment) allows you to maximize your efforts in achieving these factors. Take every opportunity to avoid wasting time on side issues, administration and regularly scheduled meetings (which often only happen because they are in the diary, not because they matter).

One very important point to consider is whether your personal objectives and the aspirations of the new owners are fully aligned. For example, you might be financially rewarded on short-term profitability but the new owners want long-term sales growth. It is often possible to boost short-term profits by cutting costs and holding back on investment. Sometimes this is achieved at the expense of longer-term growth and future profitability. If you allow this situation to arise, problems will develop, and they are not minor issues – they are structural problems that go to the heart of your business strategy. Be open, honest and realistic about joint objectives early in your discussions with potential buyers.

Be incentivized for out-performance

Earlier in this chapter we touched on the difficulties of remaining motivated whilst 'under new ownership'. This might be especially difficult if you have had the good fortune to bank a fairly large cheque upon signing your business away. Perhaps you now have enough personal assets not to have to work, but here you are back at your old desk reading e-mails from the new accounts team advising that you haven't filled in your expenses form properly! How will you remain motivated in this situation? If I were advising the person buying your business I would suggest they hold back as much of your payout as possible – for as long as possible. However, as I have already advised you to ensure the opposite is achieved, the problem remains. The answer is to ensure you remain motivated by the use of large incentives. This is not about greed, just practicalities. For example, if you were fortunate enough to bank a cheque of, say, £750,000 at the time you signed the share-sale agreement, you are unlikely to be motivated at the prospect of a £10,000 bonus in a year's time. You will probably make four or five times that amount in interest from the bank, so where is the incentive to get out of bed in the morning, let alone work hard to grow and develop the business?

Your working relationships (and peace of mind) will be enhanced if the incentives agreed for the lock-in period ensure you remain focused and motivated.

Support and promote staff

Most of the paragraphs in this chapter (perhaps the whole book) can be interpreted as being very self-serving. However, truly selfish people rarely thrive in business or any other human endeavour. Most activities, and certainly business, involve complex interactions with other people. When other people see us as self-serving they do not usually want to go out of their way to help us. In most situations, a business will have been built through the work of many people – not just the owner. In Chapter 3 I briefly considered the subject of financially rewarding staff who have contributed to your success, but other methods of reward may present themselves. For example, there could be opportunities for promoting staff owing to new opportunities arising from the sale, or there may be bigger opportunities to work in the new enlarged organization. When considering the lock-in period look – and plan – for ways to give a leg-up to others, especially in situations where everyone can genuinely benefit. This leads onto the subject of succession planning.

Succession planning

If you are locked in for two years, the implication is that at the end of the period you will leave. Of course you may not, but you certainly will have the right to. What happens to your role at the end of that time? Someone else will have to take over your responsibilities – or they might be shared amongst several people. If you are confident that you will wish to leave at the end of the lock-in, it is clearly in your interests to have your successors groomed and in place. After all, not being able to leave because there is no one to replace you doesn't sound like a good situation.

Succession planning can be very formal and involve screening internal and external candidates, or it may be very informal, based on grooming a successor, slowly allowing him or her to take more responsibility and control. The approach you choose will obviously depend on many factors, such as the specialist skills needed to handle the job, and the aptitude of people already working in the organization. Plan to plan your succession.

CONCLUSION

Where possible it is probably best to avoid a lock-in, especially if you have sold all of your shares in the business. Obviously there will be situations where having you around for an extended period makes a great deal of sense from the buyers' perspective – and often this will correspond with the seller's interests too. Perhaps the main reason for the generally negative tone of this chapter is that it is all too easy to agree to pretty much anything when negotiating the sale of your business, especially when the figures are very attractive, but the old adage 'Act in haste, repent at leisure' really does apply. Think very carefully about how you will act, think and feel when you no longer own the business and most of the resulting profit is taken by others. I'm afraid this is very much a time to think selfishly, although as Adam Smith pointed out over two centuries ago, in being selfish the business community somehow ensures that the needs of others are also met. The buyer of your business will be acting in his or her own selfish interests too – even though he or she will no doubt try to soften the perception of his or her true motives.

Chapter summary

▍ Expect to feel differently about your business following the sale.

▍ You will now have a boss – someone who will take or at least validate all big decisions.

▍ Seemingly trivial matters will probably annoy you – expected attendance at meetings or new and cumbersome administration rules.

▍ There may well be positives – perhaps more support on complex HR or finance matters.

▍ Set a time frame. Minimize the duration where possible. It is probably easier to extend if you want to stay than to get out early.

▍ Look for ways to make the lock-in more enjoyable. Pass on things you don't like doing – a chance to delegate.

▍ Take the opportunity to reward key staff by way of promotion or arguing for pay increases on their behalf.

▍ Take time for succession planning. It will be much easier to leave if you have found and groomed your successor.

10

What Next?

Imagine. You have managed your business for 10 years, spent two years planning the sale, and six months of intense and frustrating effort finalizing the deal. You have worked hard to ensure a smooth handover to the new owners and have woken up to find enough money in your bank account to last for the rest of your life. How do you feel?

What a stupid question! You feel overjoyed. Delirious. Ecstatic. Over the moon. On top of the world. Words cannot express your excitement and gratitude. At last the thing you have dreamt about and worked towards has been successfully achieved, right? Wrong.

If the people I have spoken to are typical, you are going to feel bereft rather than full of joy. That is the word several people used. Bereft.

This is a very difficult concept to grasp for those of us who have never had so much cash in the bank that we don't have to work. How can you possibly feel bereft when your time is now your own, and you have the resources to do many of the things you have always wanted to do? After all, you don't hear lottery winners saying 'I feel bereft' as they pick up the new Jaguar XJS do you? But of course I am not talking about winning the lottery. I am describing someone who set up in business and went through the pains of winning new customers and finding money to pay suppliers. Who suffered the toils of being an employer and fought cash flow battles with the bank. Who dealt with red tape and landlords, the VAT-man and petty bureaucrats. Who took calculated risks and the odd flyer, had to cajole, persuade and argue to survive, and eventually learnt to thrive. I am discussing a person who was continually in demand and took most big decisions. A person leant on by others and who suffered all of the trappings of the business owner: phone, fax, computer, mobile, desk and office and perpetual interruptions. And now? This person is now unemployed or an employee but with money in the bank.

Someone once said that 'there is nothing more "ex" than an "ex" MP'. I disagree. It can be worse to be an ex-business owner. At least MPs have their 'gong' to cuddle up with.

Of course, it's hard to feel sorry for the person who has sold a business for a large sum. They have what we all dream of, yet feel bereft. 'Get a grip,' I hear you shouting at the page. And this is what the ex-business owner needs to do. Not just to get a grip, but to firmly grasp a new routine. There is a saying that I believe originates from Japan to the effect that happiness requires 'something to do, something to hope for and someone to love'. Sounds like a reasonable recipe to me. If you think about, it your business probably provided two of these things. It certainly gave you something to do, and probably also hope (maybe just the hope of a profitable exit). At the very least you need to find something else to do.

This book has been peppered with mini case studies, covering snippets of the stories behind people who have turned a successful business into a profitable exit. What advice do they have to the newly bereft ex-business owner?

The serial entrepreneur

Tony Gill has featured throughout this book. He has shared how he launched and developed two very successful businesses. The sale of the first business in the mid-1990s generated enough cash for his family to live in comfort. However, as he was only in his early 30s, perhaps it is not surprising that he didn't put his feet up or go on the world cruise. Yet he does not feel he handled the process well and explains 'For a time after the sale I was locked into the business, and I worked just as hard as when I owned it. After all, I was a shareholder in the larger group. But it wasn't the same. It is not possible to feel the same about a business that you don't own. The motivation is different. I really did feel bereft after letting go. And however genuine and competent the new owners may be, it is hard to get used to the idea of having a boss.'

Working hard for the new owners at least gave Tony something to focus his energies on, and somewhere to go every morning. When he finally parted company with the new group he quickly jumped into new business ventures. 'I set up a property business and a machinery business, but it wasn't the same. All my working life I had focused my energies on winning new business and developing relationships with customers.' The advice he has for people in a similar position is two-fold. First, he believes you must have somewhere to go each morning. 'Have a desk, get an office, develop a routine. Do not hang around the house. Develop interests, volunteer – do something', he advises. 'But don't jump back into business on the rebound. It will take time, many months, for you to properly think through what you wish to do with your life. Don't sit around, but don't make large decisions that will be difficult to reverse.'

Tony did eventually get back into the same line of business that he had left – this time on an even larger scale. At the end of 2006 he exited his second business. Has he taken his own advice and handled things differently? 'Absolutely. I have an office – and come here each day. I am an investor in a few smaller businesses, but my role is now as mentor rather that manager. It's time to let other people take the reins and it will be fantastic to help others do well.' Does he see a time when he gets back into business on a full-time basis? 'I really don't think so. I have time for my family, for holidays and for myself. I packed 40 years of work into 20 and now want to take time for the things I enjoy. It's really no hardship doing what you enjoy.' I asked him whether loss of status and importance might be an issue. He smiles ruefully and modestly proclaims, 'Well, I seem to be doing OK at the moment, don't I?'

He does, but I think there is a lot more entrepreneurial spirit still in there.

So, Tony Gill remains involved in business but as an investor-cum-mentor rather than owner-manager. Earlier in this book I mentioned 'business angels'. Becoming a business angel can be an interesting way of remaining involved in the commercial world, whilst also benefiting from the camaraderie and support to be found in a formal network of like-minded individuals. I spoke to a member of the Yorkshire Association of Business Angels to find out the attractions for people who have disposed of a business but are perhaps not yet ready to focus solely on their golf handicap.

The business angel

Kit Bird worked in the family business until it was sold at the end of 1998. He remained involved with the business for two or three years after disposal until finally all financial and contractual obligations had been completed. Following his exit, he wanted a complete change of working environment and took up a role in the voluntary sector, working for the Prince's Trust. The role involved mentoring and supporting young people in their efforts to launch new businesses, and the scope and range of activities made for an interesting challenge.

Kit explains: 'My business had been successful, but operated in a very narrow niche. Our customers were nationally or internationally based, and I had little or no experience of businesses operating in the local economy. This presented an interesting challenge because obviously the 'start-ups' supported by the Prince's Trust generally operated at a local level. Another interesting aspect was the sheer diversity of types of business. For example, I found myself advising young people on launching retail businesses when I had no direct retail experience myself. This made the role both interesting and quite demanding.'

Perhaps this experience in supporting business start-ups motivated Kit to become involved with his local business angels organization, which he joined in 2002. Kit observed that at first he viewed the task 'in Prince's Trust mode', but quickly realized that a different perspective was required as a potential investor. Most of the opportunities offered to business angels arise from either business start-ups, or what Kit describes as 'pre-revenue businesses'. As the name suggests, a pre-revenue business is involved in research and development, or is otherwise developing a model upon which a business can be successfully launched. Banks are often reluctant to offer funding to businesses during the pre-revenue stage, preferring 'track record' to 'interesting ideas'.

Of course, picking 'winners' from the pool of pre-revenue businesses has its difficulties. Kit advises that 'a good head for figures and ability to accurately judge people' is required. The role of 'non-executive director' is very difficult to handle effectively, especially finding the balance between offering support, but not being dragged into operational activities. Kit suggests that it is rare to find a situation where a happy balance is easy to achieve. 'When investing as a business angel you generally face one of two situations. The first scenario occurs when the people running the business know what they are doing, do it competently and don't really need your involvement. They just need your cash to help them move forward, and really don't want your active support. The second situation occurs when the management team really don't know what they are doing and you have to become more involved than you would like to ensure things stay on track. Finding a happy medium is difficult, but if you are able to offer specialist advice it will always be welcome. Even experienced management teams appreciate a non-executive director who can act as a sounding board for ideas.'

Despite these challenges it appears that becoming a business angel can be rewarding in a number of ways. If you pick the right businesses to support, attractive returns can be achieved, and angels are very clear that their role is one of 'active investor' rather than philanthropist. But other rewards are available too. Becoming an angel involves being part of a like-minded community, which provides both networking and social opportunities. It can provide an interesting range of activities and opportunities for personal growth and development. At the very least you will have the chance to learn about business sectors outside of your own experience, and also develop strategic rather than operational skills. Questions such as 'How will a profitable exit be achieved?' are key to financially succeeding as a business angel.

Would Kit recommend becoming a business angel to people who have made a profitable exit from their own business and need to develop interesting ways to fill their time? 'Definitely yes, but go into it with your eyes open. Talk to experienced business angels and try to learn from their advice. In retrospect, I wouldn't have made a couple of my early investments. Everyone makes mistakes and we shouldn't be ashamed of them – in my early days I don't think I was sufficiently informed, so I did make errors of judgement.'

Becoming a business angel allows ongoing involvement in commercial activities, with very part-time commitment. However, it is not just part-time business roles that should be considered. The writer, ex-professor and ex-business executive, Charles Handy, has been exploring the themes of what he terms 'portfolio working' for many years. The idea behind the portfolio approach is that time is broken into chunks and apportioned to different activities. Some of these activities may involve paid work – perhaps non-executive directorships, or investing and mentoring in a small business. Other activities might relate to voluntary or charity work. Time might also be spent on leisure activities that have remained dormant at the back of your mind throughout a busy career. It is never too late to learn a musical instrument or develop you talent for painting.

By the way, when considering charity or voluntary work, it's easy to think of this as merely rattling collection boxes outside ASDA, or posting donation envelopes in your locality. These activities are of course extremely important and worthwhile. But there are many other ways that the voluntary sector can use your talents or experience more directly. Before setting up in business I worked for one of the world's largest and most successful consultancy businesses. Like many large organizations, it employed internal counsellors who would spend time discussing career paths, work–life balance and so on. In one meeting with such a person I mentioned that I would like to do more voluntary work, and talked about the idea of rattling collection tins. The advice that came back, however, was interesting. He suggested that I should find voluntary work that would be interesting to me, work that would 'give me something back'. At first this advice appears odd. After all, isn't the idea to give rather than receive? The point is that if you find a voluntary activity that you enjoy and are good at, you will be committed and will be a hard-working and happier person. If rattling collection tins does it for you, that's great. If not, you might become a magistrate, prison visitor, National Trust volunteer or litter picker.

One other area of activity that can benefit from the experience of ex-business people is politics. There have been a number of high-profile national politicians who entered politics after successful business careers, and local politics also attracts ex-business owners. In fact, developing an understanding and knowledge of business issues will be high up the agenda for most local authorities. After all, a significant proportion of local taxation is paid by the business community. Perhaps you have something to contribute?

For some people, therefore, part of the attraction of exiting their business may also be to leave behind the whole world of business. After all, running a business can be tiring, time-consuming and full of risk and uncertainty. Perhaps a complete change of direction would be attractive to you. Consider the case of Ray, who has featured in this book on a number of occasions. In his particular case, the most attractive aspect of a successful business exit was time to focus on a lifelong passion for sport, with a big dollop of personal development for added measure.

The health-conscious academic

Like many people who succeed in business, Ray left school at 15. Having spent most of his working life as an employee, at around age 50 he finally made the leap to self-employment. He aspired to retire at 60, whilst hopefully remaining healthy enough to pursue many interests that he had not found time for during a busy life working and bringing up a family. He was able to successfully exit his business in his 59th-year. Was retirement as easy and fulfilling as he expected?

He suggests not: 'Even though I had planned my retirement for many years, on the day I was set free my feelings were very mixed. After all, I had worked for 45 years. Work filled my days, and suddenly having no time limitations was difficult to handle. It's a mixture of things. Not earning money, not contributing. It was a strange time.'

Ray had always been interested in sport, and was a keen participant as well as a fan. Several marathon medals are displayed on his home-office wall. He confirms: 'Two things happened that finally reconciled me to a happy retirement. The first thing was that when I had been gone for a few months my old business asked me to come back to handle a project on a consultancy basis. It lasted several weeks and I really didn't enjoy it. I guess I just did it for the money, and as I really didn't need money I quickly realized it made no sense. I completed the project and vowed that I really had retired this time. The second thing that happened was that I signed up for a full-time three-year degree course in sports and fitness at my local university. This gave me something challenging and interesting to do, and filled a big chunk of my time. It has worked really well, and of course, as academic courses only take about 30 weeks a year, it leaves a lot of time in the summer for holidays.'

Does he feel that balancing time is important? 'Definitely. I have always enjoyed taking holidays, and of course they were something to look forward to during busy weeks and months spent working. When you have retired and can go where you want whenever you want, the enjoyment becomes less.' Does he have any advice for the new ex-business owner? 'Yes. Expect to feel a little strange at first, after all you life has changed significantly. Secondly, have something to do, ideally pursue several interests. As well as studying I am learning to play guitar and mess around on the golf course. Finally, don't make any long-term decisions during your first year. You need time to work out what you want to do.'

It seems that even achieving a long-term, long-planned ambition isn't necessarily as straightforward as you might have thought.

Finally, it might be worth mentioning one further approach – developing an entirely different career path. Maybe you are too young to retire. Perhaps you haven't made enough money to drop out of the world of work altogether. The nest egg provided by selling a business can be just enough to allow you to change career. Perhaps it could pay off your mortgage, which means you can take a lesser-paid job that is more fulfilling. This theme takes us all the way back to Chapter 3, where a key question was what do you want to achieve? Not everyone wants to enjoy the trappings of significant wealth. Of much greater value is having the opportunity to spend time doing what you want to do, rather that what you have to do. If beauty is in the eye of the beholder, then so is success.

I know of at least one person who exited his business and has gone on to spend a large proportion of his time writing. In fact, I know him reasonably well because he is me. For a number of years I have written articles on business topics for professional magazines, and have also contributed to music publications on the trials and tribulations of performing music as an adult. A few days after exiting my business I developed an idea for an article on the subject of valuing and selling a business. When I committed my thoughts to paper I realized there would be enough material for several articles on the subject. Finally, the thought developed further. Perhaps, just perhaps, this might make a reasonable idea for a book. But could I write a book? If you are reading this, the final manuscript avoided the publisher's waste basket. Yes. It means I wrote a book. And the music book begins tomorrow.

What will you do?

11

A Call to Action

Knowledge and ideas without communication are pretty useless. Knowledge and ideas without action are sterile, at least in the hectic and eventful world of business. I hope that this book has provided information that might be transformed (having been processed inside your head) into knowledge, and that this in turn evolves into ideas. However, converting ideas into action is a supremely difficult step. Then again you already know this. You run a business.

I first realized that the topic of selling a business generated interest one day in the office. I was involved in a meeting with someone I hadn't seen before. He ran a successful business and was very competent and articulate, and exuded energy. I mentioned that I had recently sold my business and this generated a high level of agitated interest on his part. His questions were urgent and in earnest: 'How had I sold the business? How did I find a buyer? How did I know how much to ask for? Why was I still working in the business?' I had inadvertently stumbled on a topic of huge interest and importance. In attempting to answer his questions it occurred to me that even competent and articulate businesspeople appear stuck when faced with the question of how to profitably sell a business. I tested the idea on a number of other business acquaintances and it appeared that the topic merited careful attention.

Having read this book, it might be useful if you actually do something with what you have discovered. This might begin with simply writing down a number of activities that would be involved in planning for the sale of your business – even if the disposal date is likely to be many years away. The range of activities that will move things forward is more or less endless. Perhaps you could speak to your accountant about whether your business is structured in a way that allows efficient tax planning. Maybe you should begin the process of generating positive PR for your business – building a brand and reputation. It might be that customer contracts could be firmed up or formalized in a way that better secures the revenue flow in future years. Any potential buyer would be interested in that. Work out what the key steps are for your business and take action. Taking a business to a position where it is saleable – and beyond to the point where it is sold – is not necessarily a quick process, or an easy one. It involves knowledge, ideas and information, certainly. But above all it requires action.

In an effort to stop you from putting this book down, and your feet up, the following section pulls together the key themes of the book, in the hope that a brief reminder will encourage you to act.

WHO WILL BUY YOUR BUSINESS?

Completing the activities in Chapter 1 will have left you with a list of people (or businesses) who might be interested in acquiring your company. This may include competitors, customers, employees, suppliers or the lady who runs the chip shop. Think again about why someone would be interested. Remember the concept of 'vertical integration'. Consider how you might approach these people. Will you be as direct as 'the serial entrepreneur' or does our strategy require subtlety? A successful sale will require all of the skills that you have developed whilst running your business.

VALUING YOUR BUSINESS

Your business is worth what someone is prepared to pay. In that simple statement lies the key to a profitable sale. Although you may have been disappointed to learn that there is no single universal approach to valuing a business, you should also reflect that in uncertainly lies opportunity. Perhaps the single most important point is to realize 'it's about them, not you'. You may be thoroughly fed up with running your business, and have suffered a series of setbacks. But that does not mean others will see things this way. Look at your business from *their* perspective.

While there is no correct way to value a business, a number of tools exist that will help you formulate a price range. The tool most regularly applied is the 'multiple', which is both simple to calculate and easy to understand. The problem (and opportunity) with this approach is that only two key variables are involved: post-tax profit and a multiplier.

Small changes in either can significantly affect the sale price. You should consider all lawful means to increase both. In Chapter 2 I suggested that there are only three ways to increase profit: sell more, charge more or spend less. There is a fourth. Change you accounting conventions and restate profits (obviously be careful to do so lawfully).

Use a variety of valuation methods. Doing so will help you uncover the key elements of your business that will impact on the sale value.

DEVELOP AN EXIT STRATEGY

Your exit strategy may be detailed and sophisticated, or straightforward and simple. The point is to have a strategy in place that can be modified as your business develops. Planning ahead is the key to maximizing value. The most important aspect is to focus on what you want to achieve. If you require great wealth and run a modest business, you have a lot of hard work ahead of you. If getting out as soon as possible is your prime motivator, a different approach will be required. And remember, the lower you set your financial aspirations, the sooner you will achieve them. Only you can judge what success means in your terms.

How you exit your business will also be crucial. How does a two-year lock-in sound? Are you prepared to be paid out of future profits? Do you have a desire to sell all of your shares in one hit, or would you consider remaining as a shareholder? Perhaps the best advice is that you ought to have a good reason for preferring any other option to 'cash now'. Of course, this does not mean that you don't have a good reason.

PROFESSIONAL ADVISERS

Choosing the right professional advisers is important. So is managing them. One lawyer told me that a key part of his role is to ensure the contracts can be thrown into a drawer and the client can sleep easy at night. The sale process is complicated and requires experience and specialist skills. Find the right advisers and manage them. Do you require the services of a business broker? Hopefully this book has provided many ideas about how to prepare your business for sale. Nevertheless, if the book has taught you that you don't have the desire or motivation to effectively handle the sale, it might be wise to employ the services of a professional. Chapter 4 provided ideas for selecting a good one.

MARKETING YOUR BUSINESS

Marketing is about creating value and building a brand or reputation. It involves ensuring your business is known and respected. Although a whole marketing profession has developed over the last 20 years or so, there is a great deal that can be achieved on a low-budget DIY basis. The press is hungry for interesting stories and you should not find too much difficulty in providing them. If your business is growing, relocating, signing a large contract, employing people or has won an award, it should be possible to create an interesting story.

Refresh you ideas by re-reading Chapter 5 and reviewing the press release template in Appendix A.

MANAGING THE SALE PROCESS

Finding a buyer is perhaps the single most important factor in selling a business, but the sale process that follows will throw up a range of unexpected challenges. Just because you have agreed a price does not mean the negotiation has ended; it has probably only just begun (as Karen Carpenter sang). If you have found good professional advisers the challenge is now to ensure they work together in a meaningful way to a pre-determined timescale. Managing the process is your responsibility. Understanding this simple point is crucial.

LEGAL DOCUMENTATION

If you are not familiar with the term 'due diligence' you will go through a very rapid learning experience. The process attempts to eliminate risk on behalf of the buyer, largely by passing it back to the seller. Lawyers earn their fees during this phase of the process. The legal documentation that is generated as the process proceeds may be complex, and legal terminology may fuddle your brain. Nevertheless, ensure you understand all of the implications of every document.

SURVIVING A LOCK-IN PERIOD

You may feel that signing up for a further two years is a reasonable price to pay in return for a decent cash payout. You may well be right, but don't agree to be locked into a business that you no longer own until you have thought through all of the implications. Above all, consider how you might feel. Having a boss again for the first time in years may throw up more challenges than you expect, even if he or she is fair, reasonable and easy to work with.

Selling your business requires energy and a whole raft of skills. It might involve support and advice from accountants, lawyers, business brokers and trusted acquaintances. It may also involve reading a couple of books. But above all it relies on you. Good luck, and my best wishes for a successful sale.

Appendix A

Sample Documents

PRESS RELEASE TEMPLATE (SEE CHAPTER 5)

In creating a press release, remember to use 'success' words. Focus on why the release is newsworthy. It is a good idea to refer to Chapter 5 whilst drafting your release, and to sense-check the key messages when completed.

Here is a simple template for creating a press release.

Company logo and address (letterheaded paper)
PRESS RELEASE **(VERY BOLD – LARGE LETTERS)**
DATE
HEADLINE – WHICH SHOULD INCLUDE YOUR LOCATION (BOLD)
What's new? What have you achieved? Why is it important? What does it do? Why will it be of interest to readers (listeners or viewers)? What is unique about this?
Add a quote
Finish with a key message
Getting further information – name/s and contact details

OUTLINE PROJECT PLAN (SEE CHAPTER 6)

Sketch out a project plan at the earliest opportunity. It makes sense to involve professional advisers who will be able to help you understand whether timings are achievable in your specific circumstances. The sample project plan below has been restricted to 10 weeks for the sake of simplicity; a large or complex sale could take many months.

Activity	Who is responsible	Week									
		1	2	3	4	5	6	7	8	9	10
Agree heads of terms	Both parties (assisted by legal advisers)	×									
When heads of terms are agreed		×									
Due diligence • Legal due diligence • Financial audit • Draft reports	 Lawyers Accountants Both of the above		× ×	× ×	× ×	× ×	×	×	× ×		
When due diligence is complete									×		
Taxation • Review deal structure to determine tax issues • Apply for tax clearances • Tax clearances confirmed • Taxation position confirmed	Accountants × 	× × × 	× × × 					× × ×			
When all tax issues are understood and resolved							×				

Activity	Who is responsible	Week									
		1	2	3	4	5	6	7	8	9	10
Legal documentation • Prepare legal documentation • Review document reviews	Lawyers		× ×| × ×	× ×	× ×	× ×	× ×	× ×	× ×		
When all legal documents are prepared and agreed												
Communication • Agree communication plan • Agree external communications • Weekly telephone reviews • Fortnightly meetings	All	× × ×	 × 	 × ×	 × 	 × ×	 × 	 × ×	 × 	 × ×	
When we communicate in accordance with the plan		×	×	×	×	×	×	×	×	×	×
Completion • Arrange date, venue, copy documents, witnesses, financial transaction, board meeting	All								×	×	×
When we complete the deal											×
When we announce and implement post-deal communications											×

Appendix B

Sources of Help and Information

www.britishchambers.org.uk
The British Chambers of Commerce are a series of regionally based self-funded organizations that act as 'self-help groups' for business owners. Networking events are hosted regularly and are an excellent source of advice, information and (occasionally) new business.

www.businesslink.org
The Business Link website is an excellent resource and is extremely well structured and easy to navigate. If you are relatively new to business you will find many ideas and downloads that will be useful.

www.digitallook.com
The strangely named 'Digitallook' website is an excellent resource for financial information. On the site you can access p/e ratios for hundreds of organizations.

www.iod.com
The Institute of Directors offers many services in support of independent businesses. Its website contains a significant amount of free advice, much of which can be downloaded.

www.nationalbusinessangels.co.uk
Information on business angels can be found on the national website. They may also have a local organization close to you. Business Angels for Yorkshire can be found at: www.yaba.org.uk.

Index

Index of Advertisers